MW

# MAERDY SCHOOL DAYS

Infant School – Elementary School – Junior School – Community

A Sixth Selection
for the
Third Millennium

Other book titles available
by David Owen
Maerdy Rhondda Valley
Maerdy Rhondda Fach
Mid and Upper Rhondda Fach
South Wales Collieries Volume One
South Wales Collieries Volume Two

# Dewi Sant

**Words and Music by Hawys Glyn James**

anwyd Dewi bychan
wn bwthyn bach tô gwellt,
ldydd ei enedigaeth
dd storom fawr a mellt,
wthyn Dewi'n unig
venodd heulwen braf,
ynnes oedd y tywydd
oore yn yr Haf.

Cytgan:
Dyn da oedd Dewi,
Dyn da oedd Dewi
Dyn da oedd Dewi
Dewi Dewi Sa-a-ant.
Dewi Dewi Sant.
No lashing rain or thunder-
A summer's day it seemed.

The weather it was stormy
When Dewi Sant was born,
A cold wind howled and whistled
And cheerless was the morn,
But on dear Dewi's cottage
The sunlight smiled and gleamed,

rwydrodd ef trwy Gymru
'weud am Iesu Grist,
lpu rhai mewn angen
vella'r claf a'r trist;
re Mawrth y cyntaf
awel hunodd ef,
oes o wir wasanaeth
Dewi Sant I'r nef.

Chorus:
A man so saintly
Was our dear Dewi,
Dewi Dewi Sa-a-ant.
Dewi Dewi Sant
An angel took his hand
And Dewi went rejoicing
Into that promised land.

He spent his lifetime preaching,
He showed men what was right,
He helped the sick and needy
And gave the blind their sight;
On March the first at dawning

Sant (Saint David). Hand written by Glyn James former Lord Mayor of the Rhondda Valley

# MAERDY SCHOOL DAYS

David Owen and The Maerdy Archive

Infant School – Elementary School – Junior School – Community School

Top Front Cover Photograph. Maerdy Infant School Nursery Class Saint David's Day 2002. Left to right, back row: Ethan Williams, Michael Williams, Jack Rogers, Jordan Davies, Ryan Shewell, Brandon Evans, Luke Chambers, Ben Smethurst, Nathan Marchant, Jordan Creig, Josh Butler, Rhys Thomas. Middle row: Connor Oleksiak, Rebecca Roberts, Courtney Parpworth, Leah Kinson, Caitlin Clark, Georgia Richards, Georgia Thompson, Bethan Jones, Rebecca Hadfield, Katie Roberts, Jake Semmens, Chelsea Parry. Front row: Sophie Richards, Sophie Thomas, Demi-Leigh Barnes, Kayleigh O'Flaherty, Courtney Vaughan, Casey Lee Finney, Jordan Ward, Kelsey Spure.

Bottom Front Cover Photograph. Maerdy Junior School Cup Winners 1958/59 season. Left to right, back row: Mr Llewellyn Jarman (headteacher), Roy Putsey, Michael Evans, David Vaughan, Mr William John Griffiths (sports teacher), Michael Blainey, Ken 'Bunter' Thomas, John Satherly, Mr Harold Blake (teacher). Middle row: Ken Davies, Gwilym Jones, Billy Marks, Billo Sweet, Trevor 'Pasty' John. Front row: Arfon Evans and Lyn 'Sabu' Jones.

Left Back Cover Photograph. Nine-Year-Old Pupil Margaretta Jones at the Elementary Girls School in 1933.

Right Back Cover Photograph. Gethin James, Tae Kwon Do Medallist Pupil at the Community School in 2002.

First published 2002


ISBN 0-9541057-1-0

Printed by HSW Print
Cambrian Industrial Estate, Clydach Vale, Tonypandy
01443 441100

# Acknowledgements

Thank you all for the wonderful stories and photographs relating to Maerdy School Days, which have been given to me by the people of the village. These have come from the first quarter of the nineteenth century through to the new millennium.

I sincerely thank everyone for their kindness and help. I dedicate this book to the people of Maerdy. David Owen author and archivist.

The Maerdy Archive (Registered Charity No. 1073001) Collect photographs, plans, certificates, postcards, books and artefacts, old and new of Maerdy and the surrounding areas. If you are able to assist, please contact us on 01443 732073.

# Cydnabyddiaethau

Diolch i chi gyd am y storïau a lluniau arbennig, a roddwyd i mi gan bobl y pentref, yngln â Dyddiau Ysgol Maerdy. Mae'r deunydd wedi dod o chwarter cyntaf y bedwaredd ganrif ar bymtheg lan i'r milflwydd newydd.

Diolch o waelod calon i bawb am eich caredigrwydd a chymorth. Rwy'n cyflwyno'r llyfr yma i bobl Maerdy. David Owen awdur ac archifydd.

Mae Archif Maerdy (Elusen Gofrestredig Rhif 1073001) yn casglu lluniau, cynlluniau, tystysgrifau, cardiau post, llyfrau a chreiriau hen a newydd, am Maerdy a'r cylch. Os hoffech fod o gymorth, yna cysylltwch â 01443 732073.

# Contents

# Preface

We have all been to school so it comes as no surprise that everyone holds a strong opinion of education. The trouble is that things change, and nothing changes as fast as the world in which we bring up our children. So concisely, what has changed and what has stayed the same over the years?

Strategies for teaching and learning, for caring, conduct and discipline:- Resources needed to meet the demands of the 21st Century:- The very language of education:- The Comprehensive system, and the National Curriculum:- The challenges faced by pupils and staff:- The system of National Tests and reports.

What things have stayed the same since you were in school?
The desire to learn:- A willingness to adapt to change:- The drive to constantly improve teaching and learning:- The thirst for knowledge:- The need to read:- A success rate built on previous achievements:- The high standards of achievers.

Even if you left school just a few years ago
THINGS ARE NOT THE SAME!
Education evolves rather than just changes.
This book, Maerdy School Days reflects pictorially an evolution in schools.

Mr Peter Blake Junior School Headteacher

# Rhagarweiniad

I ni gyd wedi bod i'r ysgol felly does dim syndod bod gennym farn bendant ar addysg. Y drafferth yw bod pethau'n newid, a does dim yn newid mor gyflym â'r byd rydym yn codi ein plant ynddi. Yn fyr felly, beth sydd wedi newid a beth sydd wedi aros yn ei unfan?

Strategaethau ar gyfer dysgu, gofal, gweithredu a disgyblu:- yr adnoddau sydd eu hangen i ateb gofynion yr unfed ganrif ar hugain:- Iaith addysg:- y gyfundrefn Gyfun, a'r Cwricwlwm Cenedlaethol:- sialensiau sy'n wynebu yr athrawon a'r plant:- y gyfundrefn o Brofion Cenedlaethol ac adroddiadau.

Pa bethau sydd wedi aros yr yn peth ers i chi fod yn yr ysgol?

Yr awydd i ddysgu:- Y parodrwydd i addasu i newidiadau:- Yr angen parhaol i wella safonau dysgu:- Y syched am wybodaeth:- Yr angen i ddarllen:- llwyddiant yn seiliedig ar orchestion blaenorol:- Safonau uchel y rhai sy'n llwyddo.

Hyd yn oed mai ond yn ddiweddar y gadawsoch yr ysgol
DYDY PETHAU DDIM YR UN BETH!
Mae addysg yn esblygu yn hytrach na newid.
Mae'r llyfr yma, Dyddiau Ysgol Maerdy, yn adlewyrchu'n weledol esblygiad ysgolion.

Bon Peter Blake Prifathro Ysgol Iau

# Foreword

When I was a young girl at school my father used to love to tell me how his father, John Evans, cycled from Aberaeron to Maerdy to look for work. He was a tailor and found lodgings somewhere in Maerdy where he sat cross-legged on the table to sew. When he had saved enough money he sent for his wife and five children and rented a house in Ferndale, which he later bought. My father was the eldest and came to Ferndale in 1914. He was twelve years old and went to the "Higher Grade" school where Ferndale Infants' School now stands in North Road. He didn't go to school in Maerdy. How I wish he had! I might have been able to find his name in the Admission Register. I look at the names - names that are still familiar to us in the Maerdy of 2002 and I think of the changes that the schools have seen over the years.

It has been my privilege to work in Maerdy since 1988 and to appreciate the great talent of the village and its inhabitants, both past and present. It truly is a Community, which does its best for its own. What an honour to be asked to write a foreword to this book! The author has lovingly assembled these photographs, which tell us more of the history of our Community than mere words ever could. I hope that children not yet born will one day look over these pages of the history of their schools and will thank God for the vision and dedication of David Owen and "The Maerdy Archive".

Mrs Gwyneth Maliphant Infant School Headteacher

# Rhagarweiniad

Pan oeddwn yn ferch ifanc, fe hoffai fy nhad sôn am sut yr aeth ei dad, John Evans, ar gefn beic o Aberaeron i Maerdy i chwilio am waith. Teiliwr oedd ei alwedigaeth a fe ddaeth o hyd i lety rhywle yn Maerdy, lle eisteddai gyda choesau croes wrth y bwrdd, yn gwnïo. Pan oedd wedi ennill digon o arian, danfonodd am ei wraig a phump o blant, i ddod i d roedd yn rhentu yng Nglynrhedyn, ac yn hwyrach fe brynodd y t. Fy nhad oedd yr hynaf ac fe ddaeth i Maerdy yn 1914. Roedd yn 12 mlwydd oed ac fe aeth i ysgol 'Safon Uwch' ar safle Ysgol Fabanod Glynrhedyn ar Ffordd y Gogledd. Ni aeth i'r ysgol yn Maerdy yn anffodus. Byddwn wedi gallu darganfod ei enw wedyn ar Gofrestr yr Ysgol. Edrychais ar yr enwau, enwau sy'n gyfarwydd i ni o hyd yn Maerdy yn y flwyddyn 2002 a dychmygais y newidiadau sydd wedi digwydd dros y blynyddoedd.

Mae hi wedi bod yn anrhydedd i weithio yn Maerdy ers 1988 ac i gydnabod y talent sydd ymysg y bobl, ddoe a heddiw. Dyma yw Cymuned sy'n edrych ar ôl ei phobl. Mae hi'n anrhydedd i mi i ysgrifennu y rhagarweiniad i'r llyfr yma! Mae'r awdur wedi casglu gyda chariad, y lluniau sydd yn gallu dweud, fwy na geiriau hanes ein Cymuned. Rwy'n gobeithio y bydd y cenedlaethau i ddod yn gallu pori trwy'r tudalennau o hanes a diolch i ymroddiad David Owen ac "Archif Maerdy".

Bon Gwyneth Maliphant Prifathrawes Ysgol Fabanod

# Introduction

High quality education has long been synonymous with the schools in this valley. Generation after generation of young people have benefited from this process and gone on to make significant contributions in all walks of life and undoubtedly a key factor in this has been their experiences in growing up in a close knit community where education is highly valued.

It is all too easy these days to believe that schools only exist to push their pupils through examinations. Of course this is an important part of our role, but there is so much more required to provide a basis upon which pupils can move forward in life. It is a complicated process with parents, teachers, the community and the pupil themselves all having to work together, but when it is accomplished we should all take great satisfaction from the results and considerable pride in the achievement.

Education has undergone massive changes during my time in teaching and not all of it for the better. But throughout this time there has been this one reassuring constant that all schools continue to strive to meet the needs of the individuals they serve. This book, Maerdy School Days, illustrates how the Rhondda Fach schools have met such challenges and how they have created the reputation of which we should all be proud.

Mr Peter Jenkins Community School Headteacher

# Cyflwyniad

Mae addysg o'r radd uchaf yn gyfystyr ag ysgolion y cymoedd. Mae cenedlaethau wedi mynd trwy'r broses ac wedi gwneud cyfraniad allweddol mewn meysydd amrywiol a gwahanol. Ffactor allweddol yn hyn o beth yw cael eich codi mewn cymuned glos lle mae gwerth a pharch mawr i addysg.

Mae hi'n rhwydd i feddwl erbyn hyn mai ond lle i wthio plant trwy arholiadau yw ysgolion. Wrth gwrs mae hyn yn rhan allweddol o waith ysgol, ond mae llawer mwy i addysg gan ei fod yn gosod sylfeini bywyd. Mae yn broses cymhleth gyda rhieni, athrawon a phlant yn gorfod cydweithio, ond pan fo'n cael ei gyflawni gallwn fwynhau a bod yn falch o'r canlyniadau.

Mae addysg wedi mynd trwy newidiadau mawr yn ystod fy amser i yn dysgu ac weithiau nid er gwell. Ond trwy gydol yr amser yma mae yna un peth yn sicr, mae'r ysgolion wrthi yn ceisio ateb gofynion yr unigolion a wasanaethir. Mae'r llyfr yma, Dyddiau Ysgol Maerdy, yn creu darlun o sut mae ysgolion Rhondda Fach wedi ateb y sialensiau ac wedi creu enw da y gallwn i gyd fod yn falch ohono.

Bon Peter Jenkins Prifathro Ysgol Gymuned

# *One*
# The Infant School

Maerdy Infant School opened on Monday 6 September 1880. It was run by the Ystradyfodwg School Board and the first day began at twelve o'clock with a procession from the office of the company to the school. The Hirwaun Brass Band led the way followed by colliery officials and then the children singing hymns especially learned for the occasion.

The chairman was Daniel 'Eos Dar' Evans who made a speech and declared the school open. The children were refreshed with a most substantial tea, and then two apples were given to each child distributed by Mrs Thomas, Bryn Awel, Aberdare. The most distinguished visitors were entertained to luncheon at the Maerdy Hotel and a concert was given in the evening. Seventy-eight children were admitted on Tuesday 7 September and on the Thursday the Baptist minister Revd W.T. Williams visited. The children were obviously badly in need of a school as the first headteacher records that only six children knew their letters and that the children did not understand much English. The Education provided was not free; the children were expected to pay their "school pence" which were billed to the colliery at Ferndale if they failed to pay. The first inspector visited on 1 October of that year. He found that the children were "in a wretched condition".

The Headteacher had to teach monitors first and then they taught the younger children. These older monitors then had to pass "pupil teacher examination" each year; later qualified teachers were appointed. At the end of the first year in July 1881 the inspectors reported that, "the Infants have passed a highly creditable first examination and are well disciplined."

The Explosion of 23 December 1885 was described as "terrible" and some of the survivors visited the school in May 1886 to talk to the children about their experiences.

The school was enlarged in 1907. Milk was not supplied until 1935. The entry for Monday 4 September 1939 (the day after World War Two broke out) states only that "the milk was late".

Fire broke out at the school on 18 November 1964 when the Main Hall and four classrooms were gutted. Two classes were accommodated at the Junior School and the remainder at Ebenezer Vestry, (now Teify House). The new nursery block was officially opened on 1 May 1976.

Mrs Gwyneth Maliphant Infant School Headteacher

Maerdy Infant School opened on Monday 6 September 1880. It was run by the Ystradyfodwg School Board and the first day began at twelve o'clock with a procession from the office of the company to the school. The Hirwaun Brass Band led the way followed by colliery officials and then the children singing hymns especially learned for the occasion. Assembly is held every morning. A part of the school day when all the children share a precious and momentous time together.

## The Infant School Prayer

*This Is Our School.*
*Let Peace Dwell Here;*
*Let The Rooms Be*
*Full Of Contentment.*
*Let Love Abide Here -*
*Love Of One Another,*
*Love Of Mankind,*
*Love Of Life Itself*
*And Love Of God.*
*Let Us Remember*
*That, As Many Hands*
*Build A House,*
*So Many Hearts*
*Make A School.*

*Amen.*

## Gweddi Ysgol Fabanod

*Dyma Ein Hysgol.*
*Bydded Heddwch Yma;*
*Bydded i'r Ystafelloedd*
*Fod yn Llawn Bodlonrwydd.*
*Bydded i Gariad Fod Yma -*
*Cariad Ein Cyd-ddyn,*
*Cariad Dynoliaeth,*
*Cariad Bywyd*
*A Chariad Duw.*
*Cofiwn*
*Dwylo Niferus*
*Sy'n Adeiladu T,*
*Calonnau Niferus*
*I Greu Ysgol.*

*Amen.*

The Infant Council School Class 1a in 1914. Since the school began the staff, children, governors, parents and the local people of the village have raised thousands of pounds to benefit the school and the children in their education. Thanks must be given to one and all that have given their time and help in any way, little or large, over the past one hundred and twenty years. There is a small account in the following chapter of some achievements and money raised for the school.

**The Infant School Headteachers from 1880 to date**

| | | |
|---|---|---|
| 1880 | 1882 | Lavinia Morris |
| 1883 | 1884 | Suzannah Arthur |
| 1884 | 1886 | R.E. Phillips |
| 1886 | 1896 | M. Bowen |
| 1896 | 1898 | M. Jeremiah |
| 1898 | 1903 | A.M. Davies |
| 1903 | (temp) | M.H. Williams |
| 1903 | 1926 | A. Humphreys |
| 1926 | 1945 | Miss Jessie Bull |
| 1945 | 1950 | Miss A.J. Williams |
| 1950 | 1960 | Miss Muriel Howells |
| 1960 | 1968 | Miss Blanche Richards |
| 1968 | 1970 | Miss Megan Davies |
| 1970 | (acting head) | Miss S.E. Williams |
| 1970 | 1988 | Miss Marion Bennett BA |
| 1988 | (to date) | Mrs Gwyneth Maliphant |

The Infant Council School Class 1b in 1914. A little girl aged three took the following poem home from school for her mam and dad. There used to be so many of my fingerprints to see. On furniture and walls and things from sticky, grubby me. But if you stop and think awhile you'll see I'm growing fast. Those little handprints disappear, you can't bring back the past. So here's a small reminder, to keep, not wipe away. Of tiny hands and how they looked to make you smile someday.

The Infant Council School Class 1c in 1914. The Little Ducks who live in Wales. Give us a flood of water, Let it rain tomorrow and always, Give us plenty of little slugs and other luscious things to eat, Protect all folk who quack and everyone who knows how to swim. The young author is unknown, but probably thought it rained a lot in Wales.

The Infant Council School Class 2d in 1914. The Infant School won first prize in the Infant Category in the National Pan Macmillan School Library Award designed to find the best school library in the country. Pupils and staff chose new books from the Pan Macmillan lists for their library. The school community also raised money for books and established a library as a focal point within the school.

The Infant Council School Class 2f in 1914. The school library is used by individual children, groups, classes, staff and parents. The books have Welsh and local history, information, pictures and stories, and children can browse according to their interests, find out the answers to their questions and generally develop their investigative skills.

The Infant Council School Class 3h in 1914. The school has always aimed to identify positive qualities or talents in all the children, to give them a sense of pride in their achievements and to encourage their self-confidence, self-awareness and motivation in preparation for the future and their next big step, the Junior School.

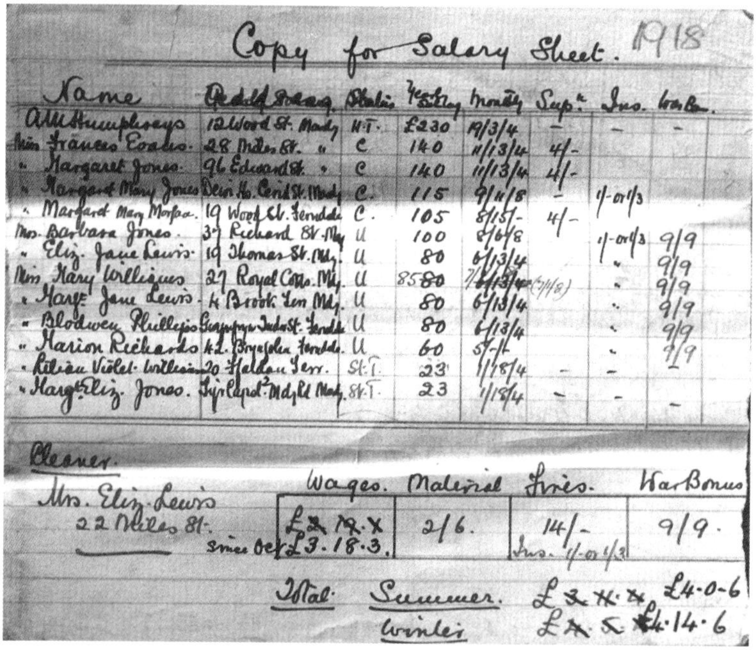

Copy for Salary Sheet. 1918

| Name | Address | Status | Yearly Salary | Monthly | Sup.n | Ins. | War Bonus |
|---|---|---|---|---|---|---|---|
| A M Humphreys | 12 Wood St. Mardy | H.T. | £230 | 19/3/4 | – | – | – |
| Miss Frances Evans. | 28 Miles St. " | C | 140 | 11/13/4 | 4/- | | |
| " Margaret Jones. | 96 Edward St. " | C | 140 | 11/13/4 | 4/- | | |
| " Margaret Mary Jones | Dein Ho. Conl St. Mardy | C. | 115 | 9/11/8 | – | 1/-or1/3 | |
| " Margaret Mary Morgan. | 19 Wood St. Ferndale | C. | 105 | 8/15/- | 4/- | | |
| Mrs. Barbara Jones. | 37 Richard St. Mdy | U | 100 | 8/6/8 | | 1/-or1/3 | 9/9 |
| " Eliz. Jane Lewis. | 19 Thomas St. Mdy. | U | 80 | 6/13/4 | | " | 9/9 |
| Miss Mary Williams | 27 Royal Cotts. Mdy. | U | 85 ~~80~~ | 7/~~6/13/4~~ (7/1/8) | | " | 9/9 |
| " Marg.t Jane Lewis. | 4 Brook Ten Mdy. | U | 80 | 6/13/4 | | " | 9/9 |
| " Blodwen Phillips | [illegible] Ind. St. Ferndale | U | 80 | 6/13/4 | | " | 9/9 |
| " Marion Richards | 42 Brynsolen Ferndale. | U | 60 | [illegible] | | " | 9/9 |
| " Lilian Violet Williams | 20 Haldan Terr. | St.T. | 23 | 1/18/4 | – | – | – |
| " Marg.t Eliz. Jones. | Tyr Capel [illegible] Rd Mdy. | St.T. | 23 | 1/18/4 | – | – | – |

Cleaner.

Mrs. Eliz. Lewis
22 Miles St.

| | Wages. | Material | Fires. | War Bonus |
|---|---|---|---|---|
| | ~~£[illegible]~~ since Oct £3.18.3. | 2/6. | 14/- Ins. 1/-or1/3 | 9/9. |

Total. Summer. ~~£[illegible]~~ £4-0-6

Winter ~~£[illegible]~~ £4.14.6

A Copy of the Infant School Staff Salary Sheet in 1918. The Infant School cleaner Mrs Lewis formally of 22 Miles Street was given a War Bonus during World War One of 9s-9d (approximately 49p). The school was awarded a prize for the outstanding standard of entries in the Royal Mail Young Letter Writer Competition. The infant school was the winner in the South Wales and South West area. Graham Jones, Royal Mail delivery area manager, presented the prize to the school at a special assembly.

The Infant School Teaching Staff in 1922. The Photograph includes: Miss Muriel Howells, Miss Lizzie Jane Dunn, Miss Bessie Jones, Mrs May Evans, Miss Frances Evans, Miss Hannah Davies, Miss Margaret Mary Jones, Miss Lilly Williams, Mrs Lilwen Richards. The school was awarded a bronze dog statuette in a competition with hundreds of other schools for helping Smiths, the crisp manufacturer raise money for the PDSA. The money was needed to buy medicines and vital equipment for the charity's animal surgeries.

Left: Odyle Evans (Thomas) Pupil at the Infant School in 1927. I went to school today and we start at nine o'clock and go home again at half past three. Our teacher is Miss Howells. She is very nice and wears glasses. Teacher marked the register, when she calls our name, we must shout "Yes Miss". We did some sums and then had our bottles of milk. After milk we went out to play. After play, teacher told us how the milk comes to our houses every day. At twelve o'clock we all went home for dinner and came back again at half past one. Teacher drew some coloured balls on the blackboard and we had to thread coloured beads onto a piece of string in the same way as they are on the blackboard. We went out to play in the yard; some of the girls had skipping ropes. When the teacher rang the bell we had to get into lines and march back into school. Then we sang some songs and Miss played the piano. Now the day is over, Night is drawing nigh, Shadows of the evening, Steal across the sky. Then we went home. After tea, my mother gave me a ha'penny, so I bought five wine gums, they last a long time and the lady in the shop gave me a piece of cardboard so I went up the mountain with it and my friend and I took turns with it, sliding down the mountain in the mud. Friday 13 May 1927.

The Infant Schools Teaching Staff in 1928. The photograph includes: Mrs Gwen Davies, Miss Bessie Jones, Miss Gladys Davies, Miss Gladys Lavis (Morgan), Miss Nonni Jones, Miss Muriel Howells, Mrs May Evans, Miss Lizzie Jane Dunn, Miss Margaret Mary Jones, Miss Jessie Bull (headteacher), Miss Hannah Davies.

The Infant Council School Class 1a 15 July 1931. The photograph includes: Miss Muriel Howells (teacher) and Miss Jessie Bull (headteacher). Kind Saint David loving, Wonderful St David caring, Special Saint David preaching, Good Saint David helping. Helpful Saint David healing. Wise Welsh dragon flying, Red Welsh dragon sleeping, Fiery Welsh dragon roaring, Fierce Welsh dragon running, Gigantic Welsh dragon snoring. Katie Corcoran Year 2 Age 6.

The Infant Council School Class 2a 15 July 1931. The photograph includes: Nonni Jones, Lewis Jones, Arthur Jones, Walter Evans, Ted Jones, Eunice Davies, Dilwyn Roberts, Dilwyn Jones, Iuean Thomas, Ivor Thomas, John Evans Miss Jessie Bull (headteacher), Glyn Jones, Joyce Davies, Brenda Griffiths, Nan Duggan, Griff Jones, Tommy Owen Jones, Richy Davies, Elfed Evans, Mal 'Bob Crier' Jones, Beryl Davies, Dilys Jones, Rhys Evans, Moira Jones, Marian James, Dora Razey, Iris Moxham, Margaret Davies, Gwyneth Jones, Marion Jones, Elined Rees, Betty Richards, Peggy (Fletcher) Thomas.

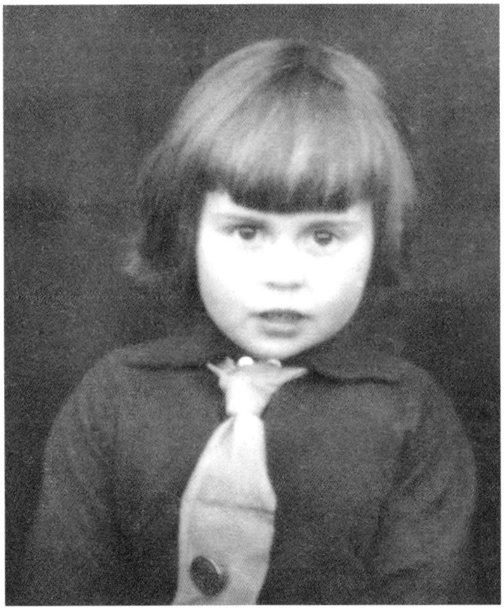

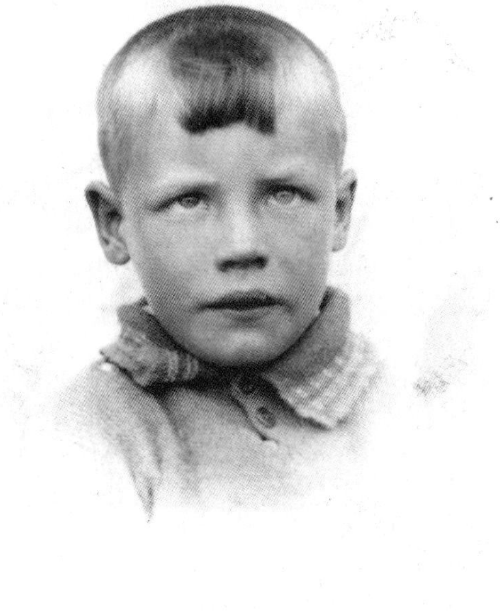

Left: Five-Year-Old Pupil Margaretta Jones at the Infant School in 1933. Right: Five-Year-Old Pupil Christopher Cripps at the Infant School in 1934. February 14th Saint Valentine's Day. We send cards to special friends. I give a card to Michael Lawes and a present to Michael. Michael gave me a card and a present. Shanice Richards Year 2 Age 6.

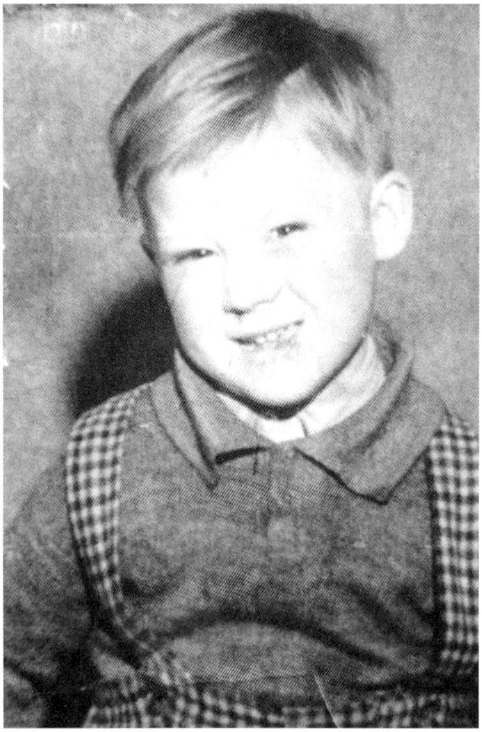

Left: The first day at the Infant School for Pupil Royston Jones in 1947. My favourite games that I played in the yards at playtime were marbles, soccer and hide and seek. I liked my milk at school. Some of the milk we drink in school and in our houses comes from the Co-op and some of the milkmen go to Maerdy Station early in the morning to meet the train. The milk men get the churns they want, some only need one churn and some have more. He then fills his milk can with a lid on it, so that he can carry it from house to house. He knocks on the doors and shouts "Milk-O". Then the ladies in each house come out with their jugs and the milkman dips his half-pint measure into the churn and pours it into the jugs. In some places the milk comes in bottles, which is a lot easier for the milkman and much cleaner.

The Infant School in 1954. The photograph includes: Miss Muriel Howells (headteacher) and Mrs Gladys Morgan (teacher). Yesterday we went to the church. It is Harvest time. We saw fruit and vegetables and a big loaf of bread. We was singing in the church and we sing for a lady from America. Demi Finney Year 2 Age 7.

The Infant School children on their way to the Junior School for their first new day in September 1954. The photograph includes: Pauline Thomas, Susan Wharton, Carol Francis, Joan Davies, Gaynor Jones, Lyn Jones, Gillian Davies, Aeronwy Evans, Lyn Morris, David Jones, Trevor John, Janice Venning, Miss Bessie Jones (teacher), Mrs Gladys Morgan (teacher).

The Infant School in 1955. Left to right, back row: Mrs Gladys Morgan, (teacher), Miss Starr (teacher), Miss Muriel Howells (headteacher). Third row: Janice Davies, Susan Thomas, Jennifer Jones, Moira Evans. Second row: Helen Thomas, Michael Hughes, Annie Betteridge, Glyn Rosser, Linda Jones, Sandra Jones, Derek Maybe. Front row: Linda Jeans, Keith Llewelyn, Lynn Morris, Linda Williams, Brian Jones.

The Infant School in 1957. Left to right, back row: Mrs Veronica Jarman (teacher), -?-?- , D. Williams, H. Morgan, T. Parry, M. Higgins, P. Evans, C. Thomas, M. Wiltshire, R. Feltham, I. Williams, A. Lawes, Miss Muriel Howells (headteacher). Third row: P. Williams, J. Mardon, A. Jones, K. Hayes, M. Beecham, S. Woodhouse, A. Davies, G. Jones, D. Williams. Second row: C. Williams, D.R. Jones, S. McCarthy, N. Williams, A. Jones, A. Jones, L. Jones, W. Piper, B. Jones, M. Jones. Front row: T. Powell, P. Wilson, G. Morris, A. Hughes, -?-?- , M. Lewis, L. Richards, M. Mullins.

The Infant School in 1959 prior to the temporary building affectionately called the Ponderosa being built. The photograph includes: Wendy Howells, Steven Aberteli, Susan Lloyd, Cheryl Jones, Olivia Jones, Anthony Lewis, Edward Thomas, Derek Ballinger, Kerry Steele, Anthony Evans, Kelvin Davies, Stuart Davies, Gillian Richardson, Alwyn Bowen, Vanessa Tann, Tina Dean, Myra Davies, Keith Jones, Barbara Mazey, Rhoslyn Howells, Ann Llewelyn, Lynda Hughes, Susan Davies, Helen Davies, Hillary Jones, Pauline Williams, Karen Lewis, Joanne Chaffe, Avril Jones, Myfanwy -?- .

The Infant School 19 November 1964. Fire broke out at the school on 18 November 1964 when the Main Hall and four classrooms were gutted. Two classes were accommodated at the Junior School and the remainder at Ebenezer Vestry, (Teify House). The new nursery block was officially opened on 1 May 1976 with bright, spacious areas where the children were able to play whilst learning.

Left: The Infant School Saint David's Day 1 March 1965. The photograph includes: Michael Gregory, Malcolm Gregory, Diane Villis, Linda Minton, David Jones. Right: Five-Year-Old Pupil Caroline Davies at the Infant School in 1966. In 1989 The Prince of Wales' Committee, Valleys Initiative Planting Programme awarded a grant of £500 to plant small trees and plants in the school grounds. The children planted and labelled the saplings and plants with help from parents and friends in just three days.

The Infant School Teaching Staff May 1977. Left to right, back row: Mrs Cynthia Mainwaring, Mrs Dawn Wood, Mrs Mary Fisher, -?-?- , Mrs Lyneth Bevan, Mrs Joan Lewis. Front row: Mrs Patricia Llewellyn, Mrs Pamela Phillips, Mrs Mary Thomas, Miss Marion Bennett BA (headteacher), Mrs Doreen Evans, Mrs Christine Carpenter, Miss Nan Jones.

The Infant School in the 1980s. The photograph includes: Miss Marion Bennett BA (headteacher), Carl Birdikin, Meirion Brown, Neil Rees, Phillip Osborn, Susan Lewis, Teresa Agg, Susan Jones, Bethan Morgan, Mrs Pamela Phillips (teacher). In June 1990 a Summer Fete was held at the school and it raised £925, which was used for the education of the children. The local shopkeepers donated the excellent prizes, and thanks were extended to them. The 'Community Spirit', of which Maerdy is famous, lives on!

The Infant School Classes 1, 2, 3, and 4 Saint David's Day 1 March 1979. The photograph includes: Amanda Richardson, Simon Evans, Tina Evans, Adrian Crabb, Kathy Jenkins, Derry Tustin, Peter Griffiths, Lisa Chapman, Sharon Crabb, Tara Davies, Rhian Thomas, Jane Pritchard, Wendy Keech, Mathew Kim, Nicola Barnes, Catherine Evans, Kerry Humphries, Lisa Kerry, Dewi Evans, Luanda Richardson, Martin Edwards, Tina Ryall.

The Infant School Classes 5, 6, 7, 8 and 9 Saint David's Day 1 March 1979. The photograph includes: C. Thomas, J. Hayes, J. Paul, J. L'Homme, C. Benjamin, J. Cronin, C. Hughes, N. Wosley, L. Maybe, C. Clements, M. Parry, N. Sikes, C. Woodington, T. Richardson, T. Haycocks, L. Jones, M. Davies, K. McNamara, N. Watkins, N. Beazley, C. Prowl, L. Carter, D. Wells, J. John, S. Burdikin, J. Davies, L. Wharton, T. Marsh, G. Inkpen, S. Watkins, G. Frances, I. Rosser, R. Stevenson, G. Jones.

The Infant School Nursery Class in 1982. The photograph includes: Mrs Cynthia Mainwaring (nursery nurse), Miss Nan Jones (teacher), Miss Marion Bennett BA (headteacher), Mrs Patricia Llewellyn (teacher). Hugh Evans, Adam Pincott, Steven Cousins, Lee Chapman, Reagan Everson, Gavin Thomas, Gary Westacot, Clayton Gill, Paul Pratten, John Paul Satherley, Lee Jones, Carl Mason, Leah Smith, Abigail Corbett, Rachel Mathews, Jamie Mathews, Catherine Fry, Kelly Lawes, Christine Woodington, Gareth John, Ryan Hunt, Lee Richards, Wayne Mullins, Ceri Davies, Robert Pugh, Gethin Ellis, Steven Mason, Dean Davies.

The Infant School Reception Class in 1982. Left to right, back row: Miss Marion Bennett BA (headteacher), Marcus Sweet, Andrew Thomas, Craig Davies, Ricky Sullivan, Paul Downie, Lee Jones, Craig -?- , Ryan Davies, Richard Roberts, Mrs Dawn Wood (teacher). Middle row: Kelly Jones, Claire Howells, Ceryn Morgan, Nathan Lewis, Mathew Cripps, Lisa Blaney, Ross Pike, Emma McFail, Teri Blake, Leanne Chapman. Front row: Claire Kenealy, Kelly Smith, Tara Hughes, Hayley Hughes, Kimberly Jones, Donna Davis, Lana Blake, Lisa Voyle

The Infant School in the 1980s. Left to right, back row: Mrs Mary Fisher (teacher), Ryan Davies, -?-?- , Richard Roberts, Anthony Cole, Ross Pike, Ricky Sullivan, Paul Dawnie, Nathan Lewis, Lee Jones, Craig Davies, Miss Marion Bennett BA (headteacher). Middle row: Claire Howells, Kimberley Jones, Lisa Voyle, Lisa Blaney, Kelly Jones, Ceryn Morgan, Emma McFail, Terry Blake. Front row: Tara Hughes, Donna Davies, Hayley Hughes, Claire Kenealy, Leanne Chapman, Lana Blake, Kelly Smith.

The Infant School in the 1980s. The photograph includes: Miss Gillian Harper (teacher), Ian L'Homme, Raymond Woodington, David Edgell, Dean Austin, Martin Jones, Carl Jenkins, Mark Broadbent, Andrew Gill, Ceri Jones, Paul Jones, Gavin Palmer, Richard Clements, Mathew Thomas, Claire Gregory, Christian Davies, Siân Kibble, Carl Bowen, Jonathan Evans, Andrew Davies, Miss Marion Bennett BA (headteacher).

The Infant School, Mrs Susan Mitchell Reception Class 20 June 1997. Left to right, back row: Mrs Gwyneth Maliphant (headteacher), Lucy England, Jade Gouvain, Leah Trimm, Heather Lewis, Kate Phillips (student teacher), Mrs Susan Mitchell (teacher). Middle row: Kirsty Phillips, Callie Thomas, Danielle Oleksiak, Stacey Evans, Shauna Lewis, Jordan Margery. Front row: Ricky Semmens, Michael Gregory, Adam Carter, Calvin Willis, Mathew Smith, Ricky Rossiter.

The Infant School, Mrs Alice Evans Year One 20 June 1997. Left to right, back row: Mrs Gwyneth Maliphant (headteacher), Steven Jenkins, Christian Addis, Ashley Thomas, Nathan Mullins, Liam Pike, Huw Davies, Calvin Hemmings, Mrs Alice Evans (teacher). Middle row: Angela Liddon, Christopher Gordon, Natalie Evans, Nathan Thomas, Martine Thomas, Liam Hanley, Nikayla Reid, Katie Rowlands. Front row: Emily Lawes, Sarah Kinson, Kate Turner, Nia Williams, Vickie Serle, Ceri-Siân Downes, Nicole Rossiter, Esther Davies.

The Infant School, Miss Claire Jones Year One 20 June 1997. Left to right, back row: Mrs Gwyneth Maliphant (headteacher), Shauna Mainwaring, Samantha Roberts, Jade Curtis, Stacey John, Amy Thomas, Ruth Rossiter, Melissa Heafield, Miss Claire Jones (teacher). Middle row: Rachel Rowe, Claire Moulding, Danielle Thomas, Natalie Cole, Stacey Mullins, Debra Cole, Katie Mitchell, Sophie Price, Rebecca Saunders. Front row: Aled Jones, Ricky Owen, Sean Warren, Ashley John, Rhys Finney, Mathew Carter, Donovan Morgan, Sean Curtis.

The Infant School, Mrs Janet Phillips Year Two 20 June 1997. Left to right, back row: Mrs Janet Phillips (deputy headteacher), Andrew Clement, Mathew Evans, Dale Evans, Jamie Evans, Jason Thomas, Ryan Davies, Christopher Smith, Mrs Gwyneth Maliphant (headteacher). Middle row: Darren Saunders, Sean Evans, Jodie Barns, Danielle Roberts, Natasha Woodington, Sasha Hoskins, Mathew Carter, Kyle Davies. Front row: Daniel Davies, Jessica Richards, Sarah Harris, Clare Evans, Chloè Light, Sarah Kinson, Raquel Earland.

**MAERDY INFANT SCHOOL**

Dear Mrs.

will be able to start school on at

Please bring your childs birth certificate on the first day.

We look forward to seeing you both.

Yours sincerely,

G.L.Maliphant.
Headteacher.

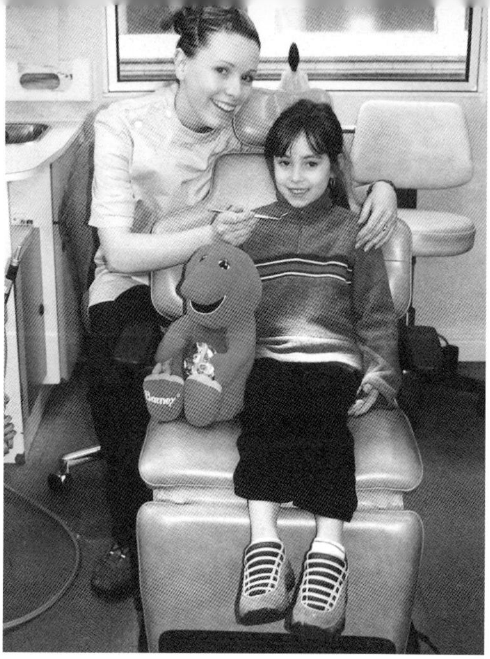

Left: The Infant School Starting Day Form. On 15 and 16 July 1998 everyone was welcomed to see the school's 'facelift' and an exhibition of the children's work. One of the highlights was the Field of Hope in the schoolyard; in memory of cancer patients at Holme Tower to mark the school's collection of £900 for Marie Curie Cancer care. Right: Dentist Miss Lowri Myrddin is checking Lauren Finney's teeth in 2000. The dentist visits the school at regular intervals during the year.

Left: Left to right, back row: Nursery Nurse Mrs Lisa Williams, Health Visitor Mrs Elaine Edwards, Charlotte Williams. Front row: Leah Roberts, Elinor Kinson, Demi-Leigh Paul in 2000. Pupils are always cheerful when health visitor Mrs Elaine Edwards and nursery nurse Mrs Lisa Williams call in to check the pupils' height, weight and eyesight. Right: Health Visitor Mrs Elaine Edwards measure John Seldon's height in 2000.

The Infant School Saint David's Day 1 March 2000 the New Millennium. The photograph includes: Emily Lawes, Sean Warren, Huw Davies, Donovan Morgan, Angela Litton, Ceri Siân Downes, Shauna Mainwaring, Danielle Thomas, Stacey John, Mathew Carter, Sophie Hopkins, Stephen Jenkins, Ashley John, Rhian Finney, Samantha Roberts, Aled James, Samantha Pain, Natalie Evans, Jade Curtis, Sophie Griffiths, Mrs Dawn Wood (teacher), Nathan Thomas.

The Infant School Children in 2001. Year Two pupils received Silver Awards for Science. Left to right, back row: H. Stephens (project officer, Education Business Partnership), Mrs Dawn Wood (teacher), Mrs Janet Phillips (deputy headteacher), Mrs Tracey Williams (teachers' aid). Third row: J. Woodington, R. Bennett, J. Hughes, M. Lawes, A. Davies, C. Williams, D. Finney, D. Paul, E. Kinson, J. Richards, D. White, M. Power. Second row: T. Hamm, C. Hood, M. Hamm, G. Curtis, K. Blaney, M. Davies, S. Pugh, T. Rogers, G. Bell, L. Roberts. Front row: S. Addis, L. Gallagher, A. Hadfield, A. Hollard, K. Corcoran, S. Richards, N. Parry, L. Thomas, S. Squire.

The Infant School Night Watchman Mr Lyn 'Sabu' Jones in 2001. I went to school today and the bell rang at five to nine. We had registration, my teacher is Mrs Phillips she is very nice. She did the dinner and packed lunch lists and collected 25p for snacks. We all sat on a lovely carpet and we talked about anything new. At five past nine we had Welsh for ten minutes then we asked and answered questions. At quarter past nine we all shared a 'Big Book' with our teacher. Then we had milk and snacks, then school prayers at twenty past ten. After this we went out to play for fifteen minutes. When it's wet we watch videos in the hall. After play we sit on the carpet to practise sums until dinnertime.

The Infant School Dinner Ladies in 2001. Left to right: Mrs Carol Jones, Mrs Nicola Curtis, Mrs Glynis Jones. Most of us stay for school dinners or packed lunch and we are looked after by four lovely ladies. Afternoon school starts at one o'clock and we have registration for five minutes. Some days we have computer lessons in the computer classroom. We have a special lady and sometimes a student to help us.

The Infant School Cleaner Mrs Mandy Comey and Caretaker Mr Kevin Hayes in 2001. Then we went out to play for ten minutes and then back in for the last lesson which was music. We learn rhythm and beat and we play drums and recorders. School finished at quarter past three and we were met by our parents. Some children stayed behind for Science Club. After tea I had £1 to spend, so I bought pop and crisps, then I phoned my friend on my sisters mobile and went up his house, and played a game on his computer. Friday 12 May 2001.

The Infant School Governors in 2001. Left to right, back row: Mr Keith Jenkins (governor support officer), Mrs Janet Phillips (deputy headteacher), Mrs Tracy Williams (teachers aid), Mrs Sandra Marsh (school secretary), Mrs Cathy Lewis, Mr Bryn Jones (chairperson), Mrs Tracy Hollard, Front row: Mrs Judith Phillips, Mrs Ann Jones, Mr David Owen, Mrs Audrey Tebbit, Mr Alfred Lawes.

The Infant School Chairman of Governors Mr Bryn Jones cutting the ribbon to officially open the school mural 17 October 2001. The photograph includes: Natasha Cowell, Luke Addis, Tiffany Davies, Jake Semmens, Courtney Parpworth, Joe Jones, Leah Beach, Natasha Hemmings, Georgia Davies, Grant Williams, Jade Hughes, Mrs Joy Rosser (Community Arts), Mr Bryn Jones.

The Infant School children at the opening ceremony of the new mural 17 October 2001. Left to right: Katie Roberts, Rebecca Hadfield, Jake Semmens, Georgia Richards, Caseylee Finney, Brandon Evans, Sophie Richards, Jack Palmer, Bethan Jones, Caitlin Clark, Georgia Thompson, Connor Oleksiak, Kieron Addis, Courtney Parpworth, Ryan Shewell, Jordan Davies, Ben Murphy, Corey Williams, Jamie Lloyd, Jorgie Kevill, Rhys Thomas, Jordan Creig, Josh Butler, Sophie Thomas.

The Infant School children at the opening ceremony of the new mural 17 October 2001. Left to right: Jason Lee, Grant Williams, Jessica John, Sara Williams, Natasha Hemmings, Sophie Evans, Adel Decino, Samantha Richardson, Liam Davies, Brandon Giles, Sam Powell, Deanna Clement, Sophie Lane, Luke Hopkins, Louise Palmer, Ashley Evans, Brett Pugh, Jade Hughes, Lauren Finney, Kyle Mathews, Jamie Evans.

The Infant School Christmas Party December 2001. Feeling Frightened. I was feeling frightened because my teacher broke her foot. I thought that she wouldn't come back to school. But when I seen her I felt happy. When she came back to school I was happy because my very own teacher came back. Amy Hollard Year 2 Age 7.

Left: Congratulations to Seven-Year-Old Pupil Sam Lee Powell with his Maerdy Mini Rugby, Players Trophy 14 December 2001. His dedication and training, earned him this special award. Right: Congratulations to Five-Year-Old Pupil Shaun Clark with his 200 Metres Distance Swimming Certificate 20 January 2002. After several months of practice, hard work and dedication, Shaun completed his 200 metre swim.

Left: Congratulations to seven-year-old Pupil Ashley Evans holding the Infant School Football Champions Trophy 2001/2002 season. Every year a football tournament is held between the infant school and the junior school. Congratulations to the team for their dedication and training practice during the year. On 11 February 2002 The Trustees of Tŷ Hafan the Children's Hospice in Wales sent a certificate of their sincere thanks to the school for raising the sum of £100 from their small change collection. On 15 February 2002 the following children were awarded a Good Work Certificate: Katie Roberts, Georgia Davies, Kelsey Hood and Grant Williams. The following children were awarded a Good Behaviour Certificate: Rebecca Hadfield, Nicole Creig, Kayleigh Pritchard, Natasha Hemmings.

The Infant School Nursery, Reception and Year One Annual Christmas Pantomime at Maerdy Community Centre 21 December 2001. Left to right, standing: Joe Jones, Machaella Finney, Tammy Mullins. Why can't every day be like Christmas? The joy of Christmas grows in our hearts, for if every day was just like Christmas what a wonderful world this would be. The pantomime was a treat to see.

Father Christmas (Siôn Corn) visits Maerdy Square Christmas 2001. Left to right: Carolyn Richards ('lolly pop' lady), Father Christmas, Jenny, Charlotte and Daniel White. Jenny and her children returning home following the infant school Christmas party. A choral evening with Maerdy Infants School Choir and the Morlais Male Voice Choir has been held at Maerdy Community Centre to raise money to benefit the school and the children in their education.

Father Christmas (Siôn Corn) visits the Infant School December 2001. The photograph includes: Sophie Richards, Bethan Jones, Corey Williams, Melanie Ward, Father Christmas, Ashley Dummer, Ryan Shewell, Demi Hughes, Chelsie Jones, Jordan Creig, Nicole Creig, Georgia Thompson, Jorgie Kevill, Nathan Marchant, Caitlin Clark, Connor Oleksiak, Ryan Harris, Phoebe Price, Sophie Thomas, Jessica Evans, Joe Jones, Chelsea Parry, Thomas Pike, Corey Mathews, Rachel Bell, Kate Israel, Adam Pike, Rhys Thomas, Charlotte White, Jessica Wiltshire, Josh Butler, Machalla Finney, Ben Murphy, Connor Hanley, Clarissa Richards, Georgia Davies, Jordan Davies, Tammy Mullins.

The Infant School Golden Awards Ceremony in 2002. Children with their Certificates for Good Work, Good Behaviour, Improved Work and Improved Behaviour on 15 February 2002. Left to right, back row: Kelsey Hood, Kayleigh Pritchard, Natasha Hemmings, Jamie Evans, Grant Williams, Joshua Wiltshire, Christopher Bell, Deanna Clement. Front row: Nicole Creig, Ashley Dummer, Katie Roberts, Ryan Shewell, Rebecca Hadfield, Josh Butler, Georgia Davies, Chelsie Jones.

The Infant School Reception Class Saint David's Day 1 March 2002. Left to right, back row: R. Harris, A. Pike, J. Nicholas, J. Kevill, C. Mathews, S. Phillips. Third row: C. Williams, C. Hanley, J. Jones, K. Addis, A. Dummer, B. Murphy, T. Pike. Second row: N. Roberts, J. Wiltshire, N. Creig, C. Richards, C. White, G. Davies, R. Bell, R. Mainwaring, M. Ward. Front row: D. Hughes, P. Price, K. Israel, C. Jones, C. Phillips.

The Infant School Saint David's Day 1 March 2002. Left to right: N. Hemmings, L. Davies, A. Evans, L. Hopkins, S. Evans, J. Hughes, J. Evans. The infant school main hall and class rooms are splendidly decorated and the nursery unit at the school is bright with spacious areas, sparklingly painted in a rainbow of colour, showing off children's work and paintings, which catch and hold the sun, the children are able to play whilst learning. It has a warm and friendly welcome for all young new starters. The children at Maerdy are fortunate enough to be starting their school days in a bright and spacious nursery unit. It must be very great fun to be three or four year old and able to spend your day in such a splendid place.

## From My Diary

Today is 1st March.
It is Saint David's Day.
We had a concert.
We sang Welsh songs.
Nursery and reception joined us.
I was wearing a Welsh shirt.
This afternoon we are going to Teifi House.
We are going to sing Welsh songs.

Gareth Bell Year 2 Age 6

## From My Diary

We dress up as Welsh ladies and rugby players.
Saint David died on March 1st that's why we celebrate
On March the first.
The girls were wearing a hat and pinnies and skirts.
The boys were wearing a Wales Rugby shirt and black
shoes and jeans or ordinary trousers. The people always
dress up on Saint David's day in Welsh clothes and we go down to Teify
House. We sing songs for the old couples.
On Saint David's Day daffodils are special flowers and leeks are.
We celebrate for Saint David's Day. We buy Welsh tee shirts
with Wales on and we got original trousers or jeans to play rugby.
I dress up as a Welsh Lady and my friend Demi dressed up as a
Welsh lady too.

Amy Hollard Year 2 Age 7

## From My Diary

Yesterday we went to All Saints church.
It is Harvest time.
We saw fruit and vegetables and a big loaf of bread.
My grandma and grandpa go to that church.
I went with them on Sunday.
I saw the big loaf of bread.
I help them make it.

Amy Hadfield Year 2 Age 6

# *Two*

# The Elementary School

The following Elementary Boys School Chapter is dedicated to Mr Gethin Jones. Gethin spent all his school days at Maerdy Infant School and Maerdy Elementary Boys School. Gethin will always be remembered for his Love of Maerdy and his Community Spirit. We share some of his fond and amusing memories of his Maerdy School Days for all to enjoy. Gethin Jones 1928-2002.

Having spent the previous four years at Maerdy Infants School, I started in the Elementary Boys School in 1935, aged seven. My first teacher was David Evans nicknamed 'Dai Paich'. The most exciting thing that happened to the class in 1935 was the 25th Jubilee of King George V. This we celebrated in great style with a tea party in each classroom provided by the teacher and his wife. We were all presented with a commemorative mug and sent home early.

In 1939 a school concert to be broadcast on the BBC was planned, what excitement! There were rehearsals in Bethania Chapel with its beautiful pipe organ. The Elementary Boys and Girls School were to take part. William David Evans, our music teacher played the organ and we were conducted by Mr W. Griffiths our headmaster (They were both past conductors of Treorchy Choir). There were very few radios (or wirelesses as they were then called) in Maerdy at that time. People who were able to afford them bought them to hear the school concert and the World Heavyweight Championship between Tommy Farr and Joe Louis.

During this time everyone seemed to have a nickname, both teachers and pupils, e.g. 'Snipe', 'Sparrow', 'Sheeps', 'Teg', 'Cochin', 'North', 'Cwat'. 'Tonky' was one teacher who came to school on a penny-farthing bike, 'Baby Elephant' was our Welsh teacher, 'Fuzzy Wuzzy' from Richard Street was also a scout for Birmingham City Football Club. We had a very good sports master in 'Dai Dan' Morgan, we also had excellent runners in the school, one being Dai Jones 440 yards, John Agg, Elwyn Teg and Walford Jones. I ran in a 100 yards race with Elwyn Evans against Ferndale Senior School, in the team was the famous Film Star Stanley Baker.

About this time evacuees came to Maerdy. They were brought to school and people came and took them to their allocated homes. There were the Mancini brothers, whose father was a British Boxing Lightweight Champion; he presented the school with the 'Mancini Cup' to be presented at sports days. Some were from London, mainly East Ham and West Ham. The Taylor brothers came from Birmingham and stayed with Vanw and Shink Evans. One of their teachers was Mr Wellington so he automatically got called 'Wellington Bomber' as the war was still on. He was shortly called back and joined the RAF. Sadly; he was shot down and killed over Germany. One of the evacuees who came to Maerdy was Joe Ball remaining in Maerdy to this day; he married a local girl, Eileen Care, and is a pillar of the community and faithful Christian.

Our Headmaster in the last two years at school was Mr Thomas 'Little Hand' Jones; he started using the system of monitors and prefects. The first head prefect at the time was Dougie Thomas formerly of Oxford Street, when he left I became head prefect.

I left the Elementary School in 1942 aged fourteen.

Gethin Jones

A sketch of Maerdy Elementary School by local artist Mr Ken Williams. The Elementary School opened on Monday 6 September 1880. It was run by the Ystradyfodwg School Board and the first day began at twelve o'clock with a procession from the office of the company to the school. The Hirwaun Brass Band led the way followed by colliery officials. The school had mixed classes. In 1889 the school had separate facilities for girls and boys, the girls using the southern or Ferndale end of the building.

The Bell in the Bell Tower (top right) fell into the yard at 9 o'clock in the morning when it was ringing for the start of a school day. The junior pupils used the front yard to go into school; the bell fell from its tower onto the yard and down the steps of the small front gate, hitting Glyn Griffiths formerly of Oxford Street, Maerdy, on the head. This caused a great commotion; Glyn was rushed off to the surgery and detained in hospital for a short period of time. He soon got over it, and became something of a hero.

Our Headmaster in the last two years at school was Mr Thomas 'Little Hand' Jones; he started using the system of monitors and prefects. The first head prefect in my time was Dougie Thomas also formerly of Oxford Street, when he left I became head prefect. My first tussle was with my own neighbour Elwyn Evans who was having a go with some lads in the yard. I was privileged to present 'Tonky' and Mr David Evans on their retirement from teaching also Mr John Henry 'Baby Elephant' Lewis on his promotion to Headmaster at Porth School.

Our teachers at the Boys School were quite a varied lot, the nicknames that we found for them, 'The round', 'The long', 'The short'. One was 'Fuzzy Wuzzy' because of his bushy moustache, 'Baby Elephant' took us in our Welsh class, 'Watty' was our Headmaster with warts around his face and if we were to misbehave 'Dai Dan' put us in our place, Mr John Evan 'Tonky' Thomas taught us History he was our favourite type, He rode his way to Maerdy on a Penny Farthing bike, Mr John David Morgan was our Maths man he fought in World War One, commonly called 'Shell Shock', but not just for fun, Mr Wellington came from Birmingham to chaperon evacuees, We gave him the name of 'Bomber' which really seemed to please, Suddenly he was called back to the skies, The next we heard was of his sad demise, Mr Vincent Evans was our reading man, Treasure Island was his theme, We spent long Friday afternoons, perusing his favourite dream, Our teacher in Dramatics and other subjects too, was Mr Daniel Hayden Davies who did quite well and so, became a well known name in local BBC, He taught us Welsh and Elocution too, while coaching, he made us realise that we could do it too, Mr Stanley Williams nicknamed 'Mutto', one day saw the air turn blue, He had an inkwell thrown at him, which caused such a hulla balloo. Gethin Jones.

The Elementary Boys School Certificate awarded to Abednigo Davies formerly of Maerdy Road who passed in the Fourth Standard 8 July 1884. At this time Maerdy as a village had been well placed and laid out with it's streets of houses running parallel with one another with the exception of a few cross streets between. It was a prosperous and happy village, an El Dorado for the miners. All the miners working at Mardy Pit were the owners of their own houses. Their children were fortunate to be receiving the best education that Rhondda could offer.

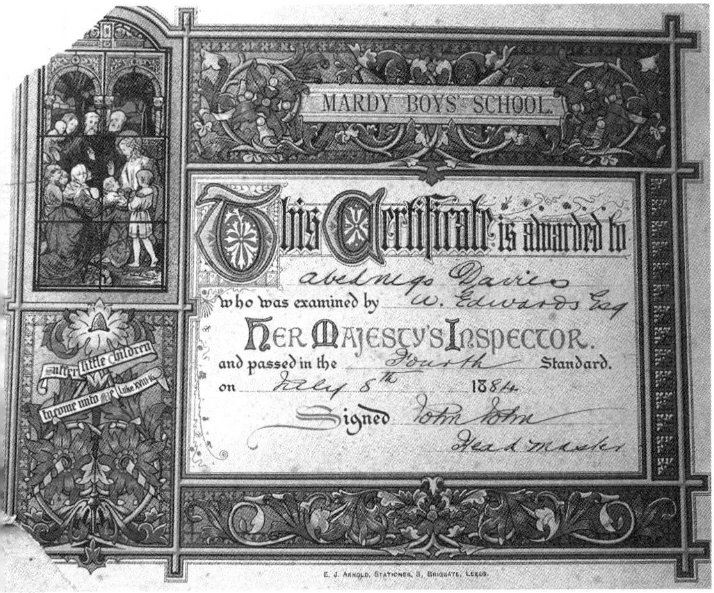


When I came home from school I dived into my tea with great haste. Only the swings and the play area in the park were on my mind. Mam I'm going up the park was a frequent cry in our house when I was a youngster. These trips were made easier with the aid of a 'Hook and Wheel'. The road in front of the park was called Office Road where the old colliery offices were. To the side were the Park Huts; the Police Station was next to these and then All Saints Church on the corner. The road at the back if the park is called 'Jubilee Walk' and was popular with courting couples. There were four entrance gates into the park, one on the nearest side to Station Terrace, one leading from what we called the 'Flower Park' into the swings and play area; this one was called the Kissing Gate. On the same railings coming out onto the swings was another gate. The main gate was at the front nearest the church. There were two pavilions one at the back of the tennis courts where bowls teas etc. were made. The other had two shelters, one facing the bowling green the other facing the tennis courts. The two tennis courts were well used and the park keeper from his little office issued tickets. At the toilet end of the pavilion and right outside the Bowling Green was a World War One Cannon, which the children of Maerdy enjoyed playing on. It was a great favourite and quite a feature. This was removed in 1942 for use as salvage for World War Two. Gethin Jones.

**The Elementary Boys School Headteachers from 1880 to 1948**

| | | |
|---|---|---|
| 1880 | 1886 | Mr John John |
| 1886 | 1893 | Mr Walter Parfitt |
| 1893 | 1913 | Mr Gwilym Lewis |
| 1913 | 1930s | Mr David Leslie Williams |
| ? | ? | Mr John Hughes |
| ? | ? | Mr W. Griffiths |
| ? | 1948 | Mr Thomas Jones |

On 24 May 1948 a fire destroyed the school and all its contents including the log books.

The Elementary Boys School in 1923. Pupils and Staff lined up in the front playground. Games played to pass time and cost nothing in the 1920-30s. One game was ‘Cattie and Dog’- a type of cricket or baseball. An old mandrel handle had about 8 inches cut of the end and was sharpened at both ends to a point. This was called a ‘catty’. The longer handle was called the ‘dog’ and used as a bat. Gethin Jones.

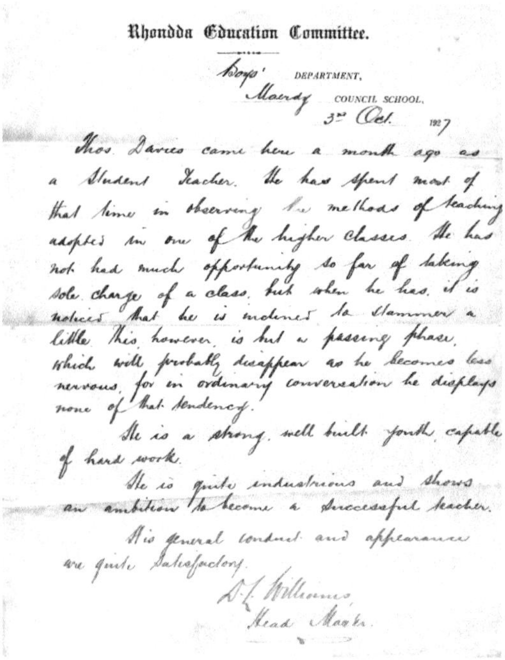

Rhondda Education Committee.

Boys' DEPARTMENT,
Maerdy COUNCIL SCHOOL,
3rd Oct. 1927

Thos. Davies came here a month ago as a Student Teacher. He has spent most of that time in observing the methods of teaching adopted in one of the higher classes. He has not had much opportunity so far of taking sole charge of a class, but when he has, it is noticed that he is inclined to stammer a little. This, however, is but a passing phase, which will probably disappear as he becomes less nervous, for in ordinary conversation he displays none of that tendency.

He is a strong, well built youth, capable of hard work.

He is quite industrious and shows an ambition to become a successful teacher.

His general conduct and appearance are quite satisfactory.

D.L. Williams,
Head Master.

Left: A letter to Thomas David Davies formerly of 29 Excelsior Terrace, Maerdy, from Rhondda Education Committee 3 October 1927. The letter reads: Thos Davies came here a month ago as a Student Teacher. He has spent most of that time in observing the methods of teaching adopted in one of the higher classes. He has not had much opportunity so far of taking sole charge of a class, but when he has, it is noticed that he is inclined to stammer a little. This however, is but a passing phase, which will probably disappear as he becomes less nervous, for in ordinary conversation he displays none of that tendency.

He is a strong, well built youth capable of hard work.

He is quite industrious and shows an ambition to become a successful teacher.

His general conduct and appearance are quite satisfactory.

D.L. Williams Head Master.

The Elementary Boys School Winners of the Rhondda School Boys Football Shield in 1927. The photograph includes: Jackie Risoli (professional footballer for Brighton), Mr John Henry 'Baby Elephant' Lewis (teacher), Mr David Leslie Williams (headteacher), Mr Rhys 'Cogman' Jones (teacher), Mr Evan John 'Tonky' Thomas (teacher), Mr John David 'Shell Shock' Morgan (sports teacher).

The Elementary Boys School Teaching Staff in 1931. The photograph includes: Mr Gilbert 'Iron Chest' Davies, Mr Vincent Evans, Mr Daniel Haydn Davies, Mr Rhydian Jones, Mr David 'Bryngwyn' or 'Dai Paich' Evans, Mr David Daniel 'Dai Dan' Morgan, Mr Stanley 'Mutto' Williams, Mr David 'Dai Lewis Barber' Lewis, Mr David Thomas Davies, Mr Evan John 'Tonky' Thomas, Mr W.B. 'Fuzzy Wuzzy' Davies, Mr David Leslie Williams (headteacher), Mr John David 'Shell Shock' Morgan, Mr William David 'Will Dai' Evans, Mr John Henry 'Baby Elephant' Lewis, Mr Geraint Lewis.

The Elementary Boys School Standard 2a (the entry class) in 1931. The Photograph includes: Hywel Williams, Eirfyl Davies, David Thomas Davies (teacher), Ollie Wharton, Stan Stokes, Mr David Leslie Williams (headteacher). When the striker hit the end of the 'cattie'. It would bounce off the floor and he would hit it as far as possible.

The Elementary Boys School Standard 2b in 1931. The Photograph includes: Mr Vincent Evans, (teacher), Arthur Webb, Jack Richard 'Milgi' Lewis, Vic Thomas, Len Hunt, Stan 'Swansea', Mr David Leslie Williams (headteacher). He got 3 strikes, and a miss was counted as a strike. Should a fielder catch the 'cattie' before it hit the ground then the striker was out.

The Elementary Boys School Standard 3a in 1931. The photograph includes: Arthur Illingworth Davies (killed in the RAF in 1944), Walter Williams (GP), Ernie Flook, Daniel Haydn Davies, John Aeron Lewis (headteacher of the new junior school 1973/1984), Mr David Leslie Williams (headteacher), Brenig Jones (POW Japan).

The Elementary Boys School Standard 3b in 1931. The photograph includes: Mr Evan John 'Tonky' Thomas (history teacher), Mr David Leslie Williams (headteacher). At the completion of 3 strikes the fielder would throw the 'cattie' as near as he could to the base (dab). If the 'cattie' landed less than the 'dog' length from the dab, the striker was out. Or, if the fielder hit the dab with the 'cattie' he was out and the next striker went in.

The Elementary Boys School Standard 4a in 1931. The photograph includes: Mr David 'Bryngwyn' or 'Dai Paich' Evans (teacher). He was given this nickname on account of the plus fours he sometimes wore, he was also known as Evans 'Bryngwyn', Meiron Teg, Mr David Leslie Williams (headteacher).

The Boys Elementary Boys School Standard 4b in 1931. The photograph includes: Mr Stanley 'Mutto' Williams (teacher), Mr David Leslie Williams (headteacher). 'Cattie and Dog' scoring was measured by using the dog length between the distance from where the 'cattie' landed to the dab. Each length of the dog was one score or, as in cricket, one run. Any number of players was allowed as long as sides were even. The highest score was the winner. With this game the only peril was a black eye or a broken window. Gethin Jones.

The Elementary Boys School Standard 5a 'The Scholarship Class' in 1931. They had just sat the 11 plus examination. The photograph includes: Mr Stanley 'Mutto' Williams (teacher), Mr David Leslie Williams (headteacher). A well known saying in the village was, we can play anything from 'cattie' and dog' to 'bull rag'.

The Elementary Boys School Standard 5b in 1931. The photograph includes: Mr David Daniel 'Dai Dan' Morgan (teacher), Mr David Leslie Williams (headteacher). The school had gas lighting, which gave a warm glow to the class room during the dismal winters, heat was provided by Tortoise Shell stoves surrounded by bottles of frozen milk in the icy winters, and part of the caretaker's duty was to keep each room supplied with buckets of coal.

The Elementary Boys School Standard 6a in 1931. The photograph includes: Mr John Henry 'Baby Elephant' Lewis (teacher), Ivor Screech, Alfred Lawes, Mr David Leslie Williams (headteacher). We used to have the same teacher throughout our junior education in the school. So Mr T.H. Davies was my class teacher for the next four years. Most of my junior school education took place in a classroom at Seion Chapel Vestry. Haydn Styles.

The Elementary Boys School Standard 6b in 1931. The photograph includes: Mr Gilbert 'Iron Chest' Davies (teacher), Mr David Leslie Williams (headteacher). The Elementary Boys School caretaker was Mrs Martin formerly of Royal Cottages and village milkman William Lewis Edwards formerly of James Street delivered the children's one third of a pint of milk to the school.

The Elementary Boys School Standard 7 in 1931. The photograph includes: Mr William David 'Will Dai' Evans (teacher) taught English and Maths 'with severe efficiency', Mr David Leslie Williams (headteacher). In 1893 Mr Gwilym Lewis educationalist musician and freemason was appointed headteacher of the Maerdy Elementary Boys School being one of the youngest men in the Rhondda to obtain such a position. Pupil Roy Lewis was awarded a wristwatch for completing seven years at school without missing a day.

The Elementary Boys School Standard EX7 in 1931. The photograph includes: Mr Daniel Haydn Davies (dramatics, welsh, elocution teacher), Edgar 'Sox' Jones, Mr David Leslie Williams (headteacher). Boys in Standard EX7 were left in school beyond the usual leaving age. Probably they were intelligent boys who had sadly failed the 11 plus exam.

The Elementary Boys School in 1932. When I moved down to the boys' school at seven years of age I began to enjoy my education. Strange, really, because my teacher was a very strict disciplinarian. Mr T.H. Davies lived in 59 Richard Street, as did four other teachers at the school, Mr Thomas Daniels (89), Mr Daniel Haydn Davies (36), Mr Vincent Evans (49), and Mr 'Will Dai' Evans (100). Mr. John Henry Lewis lived in 2 Glanville Terrace. None of the boys wanted to go into 'Will Dai's' class because he was very strict indeed. Hayden Styles.

Left: William Henry Williams Pupil at the Elementary Boys School in 1933. 72 Edward Street (brother to Beryl Davies). What can I remember about those Maerdy School Days? I know I had the cane on occasion but not as often as some of the others. I can remember some great lads, though to be honest, I never really made pals that easily, partly because I was down the bottom end of Maerdy while most of the characters I would like to associate with were from the 'top streets'. Ronnie Griffiths, Ronnie 'Sox' Jones (his elder brother was a stroke - playing opening batsman for the Maerdy Cricket Team), Donnie Lawes, Ronnie Belcher, Eddie Gregory, Evan David Lewis and the other Ronnie Jones, who I will always recall as the boy who lost his temper in class one day and threw an inkpot at the teacher. My bottom feels sore just thinking about the tanning he had - and he had a tanning from his Dad when he, having come up to 'settle the teacher', found out what had really happened in class that day. I believe he, Ronnie of inkpot fame, ran the garage opposite White Huts for a time. Indeed may even have owned it. Haydn Styles.

The Elementary Boys School Sports Winning Team in 1938. Left to right, back row: Mr W. Griffiths (headteacher), Glyn Williams, Ernie Williams, Cyril Pike, Emrys Evans, Gwynfor Richards, Bobby Owen, Mr David 'Bryngwyn' or 'Dai Paich' Evans (teacher). Middle row: Evan Davey Evans, Norman Thomas, David Connolly, Mike Hughes, David Burke, Ronnie 'Socks' Jones, Johnny Agg, Mr David Daniel 'Dai Dan' Morgan (sports teacher). Front row: Tom Belcher, Eric Davies, Billy Parry, Royden 'Sparrow' Jones, Elwyn 'Teg' Williams, Walford 'Sheeps' Jones, Harry 'Breck' Jones, Gilbert Lockyer, Bob 'The Crier' Jones.

The Elementary Boys School at Saint Athans Boys Camp in 1938. In the photograph is Mr David 'Dai Lewis Barber' Lewis (teacher). We also had excellent runners in the school, one being Dai Jones 440 yards, John Agg, Elwyn Teg and Walford Jones. When we first had sports day I remember us all piling into a 'Double Decker' bus to go to Wattstown. I ran in a 100 yards race with Elwyn Evans against Ferndale Seniors, in the team was our famous Film Star Stanley Baker. Gethin Jones.

Maerdy Boys' School

SPECIAL CERTIFICATE

FOR GOOD ATTENDANCE

During the Quarter ending 30th Sept., 1938
the School was opened 87 times
Alfred John Williams
was present 87 times.

W. J. Hughes HEAD TEACHER

The "A L" Series. E.J. Arnold & Son. Ltd. Leeds Glasgow & Belfast

The Elementary Boys School Special Certificate for good attendance awarded to Alfred John Williams 30 September 1938. Mr Shadrach Price of Maerdy was deputy headteacher for forty years. He had seen Maerdy grow from a few cottages to a bustling village. His family had been among the earliest to settle in the neighbourhood and were always associated with every movement in the locality.

Left: Mr John Morgan School Whipper In (Attendance Officer) in 1948. 'Keep your eyes out boys the whipper in is about'! His job was to keep pupils from 'mitching' or 'bunking' school (being away without permission). During the depression of the 1930s the best talents of our schools after passing their examinations had to seek work elsewhere leaving only the young and old behind. But the school children of Maerdy were still the best talent in the valley although their fathers were out of work and on the 'Dole'. The sidings of Mardy No. 1 and No. 2 Collieries had been left to go to rack and ruin. It was the proud boast of the Colliery Company that the Mardy Colliery sidings were the best in the valleys where thousands of wagons were kept full of coal ready for the market and when orders came for coal they had thousands of tons of the best marketable coal ready to sell at their own price. They were able to save wayleaves and dock dues by having such a fine large siding to stock their wagons. At one time the company made as much as 100% profit on their workings. Today wildlife is reclaiming many of the areas, attracted by a community woodland and a cleaner river.

# My Elementary School Days In 1943

The morning was bright and cold
As I set off down the road
Frost covered everything around
Like a blanket of cotton wool on the ground
Sliding along the slippery road chatting and laughing devoid of time
Oh what fun not a care in the world? Who cares about reaching school on time?

The school bell rings we're late again
Mr Evans our teacher was angry once more
Green mark for you he bellows out, clutching his cane
It cracks on our hands one, two, three and finally four.
To our desks our hand all sore we go, numbed by cane and tingling frost
Fingers too sore to hold a pen, but school work must be done at any cost.

Prayers are said to ask our lord, a psalm, perhaps a hymn
To guide and guard us through the day then our lessons will begin
Times tables are chanted and poems read,
A story from our teacher, who gives us sound advice
A little break, with hands on our head
Then its milk time, it's frozen, but nice.

There is a war on, as we all know, the posters tell us we must save
To buy some tanks and aeroplanes to send with our dads on the next wave.
Save lots of things, paper, books and jam jars
All targets for the war must be met
Our school is in the vanguard
The targets will be met.

Gas mask practice is such fun, heading for the shelters along the wall
As we march out from the school and then straight back to the hall
School meals at Bethania the chapel right next door
We also pick up rations of cocoa to take home galore
But most never got there, for it's a lovely treat
Cocoa mixed with sugar, so sweet, a treat to eat.

Crafts were most important all afternoon we spend
Making paper lanterns, chains and calendars to give to our families and friends
Evening draws nearer gas light begin to shine
As we all prepare, and anxiously wait for home time
A prayer of thanks for what we do and say
We make our journey homeward, and await another day.

Cullen Morris Age 66 of Wood Street

The Elementary Girls Council School Standard 3a in 1906. The photograph includes: Veronica Spooner, May Spooner, Annie Margaret Morgan, Lizzie Roberts, May Leyshon, Bonnie Lewis, Mrs Jane Davies (teacher). Present at the opening of the school on Monday 6 September 1880 included: Revd W. Morris (Treorchy), Lewis Davies Esq (Ferndale coalowner), Griffiths Thomas Esq (colliery manager), William Thomas Esq (colliery board) and W. Evans Esq (Bodringallt colliery). In the evening a concert was held at the Maerdy Hotel under the presidency of D. Rosser Esq. In 1889 the school had separate facilities for girls and boys, the girls using the southern or Ferndale end of the building. In 1894 the school was enlarged to accommodate the growing number of pupils from the village. Prayers were said and Hymns were sung in the classroom each morning before the daily lessons began. The following is one of the hymns that the children sang at the Elementary Girls School in 1935.

## A School Hymn

*In The Paradise Of Jesus*
*There Are Many Homes Of Light,*
*And They Shine Beyond The Darkness*
*With A Radiance Clear And Bright;*
*O That I May Hear The Angels*
*Singing O'er The Crystal Sea,*
*And Amidst Of Many Mansions*
*Find A Home Prepared For Me.*
*There Are Sounds Of Many Voices*
*In The Golden Streets Above,*
*Filling All The Air With Gladness*
*Tendered In Eternal Love.*

## Emyn Ysgol

*Ym Mharadwys Iesu*
*Mae Nifer O Gartrefi Gloeuedig,*
*Yn tywynnu tu hwnt I'r Tywyllwch*
*Gyda Disgleirdeb Glan A Chlir;*
*O Pe Clywn Yr Angylion*
*Yn Canu O'r Moroedd Mawr,*
*Ac Ymysg Yr Aml Blastai*
*Darganfod Cartref I Mi.*
*Mae Yna Aml Leisiau*
*Yn y Strydoedd Auraidd Uwchben,*
*Yn Llenwi'r Awyr A Llawenydd*
*Tynerwch Cariad Tragwyddol.*

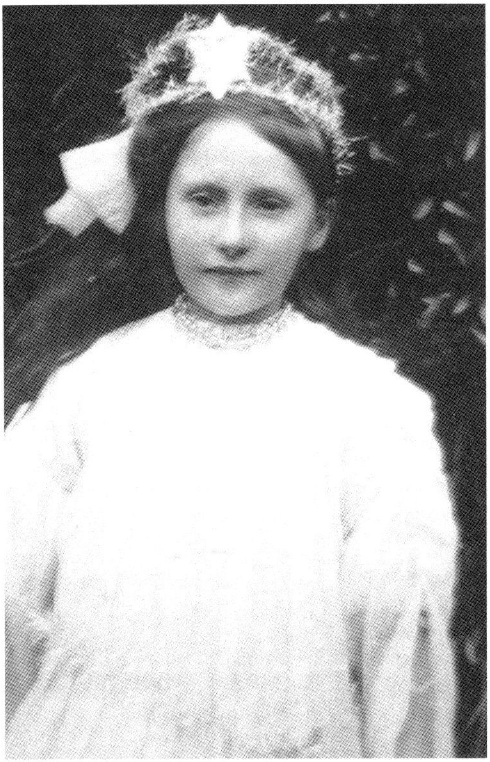

Left: May Spooner Pupil at the Elementary Girls School in 1919. Right: Beryl Davies Pupil at the Elementary Girls School in 1928. A new school was built behind Pentre Road in 1880 for the infants and all the buildings at the Elementary School were used by the older children. At that time Miss Suzannah Arthur was the headmistress of the Elementary Girls School and Mrs R.E. Henry the second wife of the Revd Joss Henry Minister of Siloa Chapel was mistress of the Infant School from 1884 to 1886. Mrs Henry's maiden name before the marriage was Miss R.E. Phillips. May the children follow on in footsteps of the old fathers and mothers and help to keep Maerdy. Although it's only a small village, it has given to the world men and women of until yence equal to any place of its size during its years of existence. Some are in Canada, USA, South Africa and on the other continents, and there are thousands in good positions in the cities and towns of England such as London, Birmingham, Wolverhampton, Coventry and Bristol etc. for talent of every description. Anthony Lewis.

**The Elementary Girls School Headteachers from 1880 to 1948**

| | | |
|---|---|---|
| 1880 | 1893 | Miss Suzannah Arthur |
| 1893 | 1900 | Miss A. Davies |
| 1900 | 1920 | Miss C.E. Davies |
| 1920 | ? | Miss Catherine Evans |
| ? | ? | Miss Margaretta Evans |
| ? | 1948 | Miss Griffiths |

On 24 May 1948 a fire destroyed the school and all its contents including the log books.

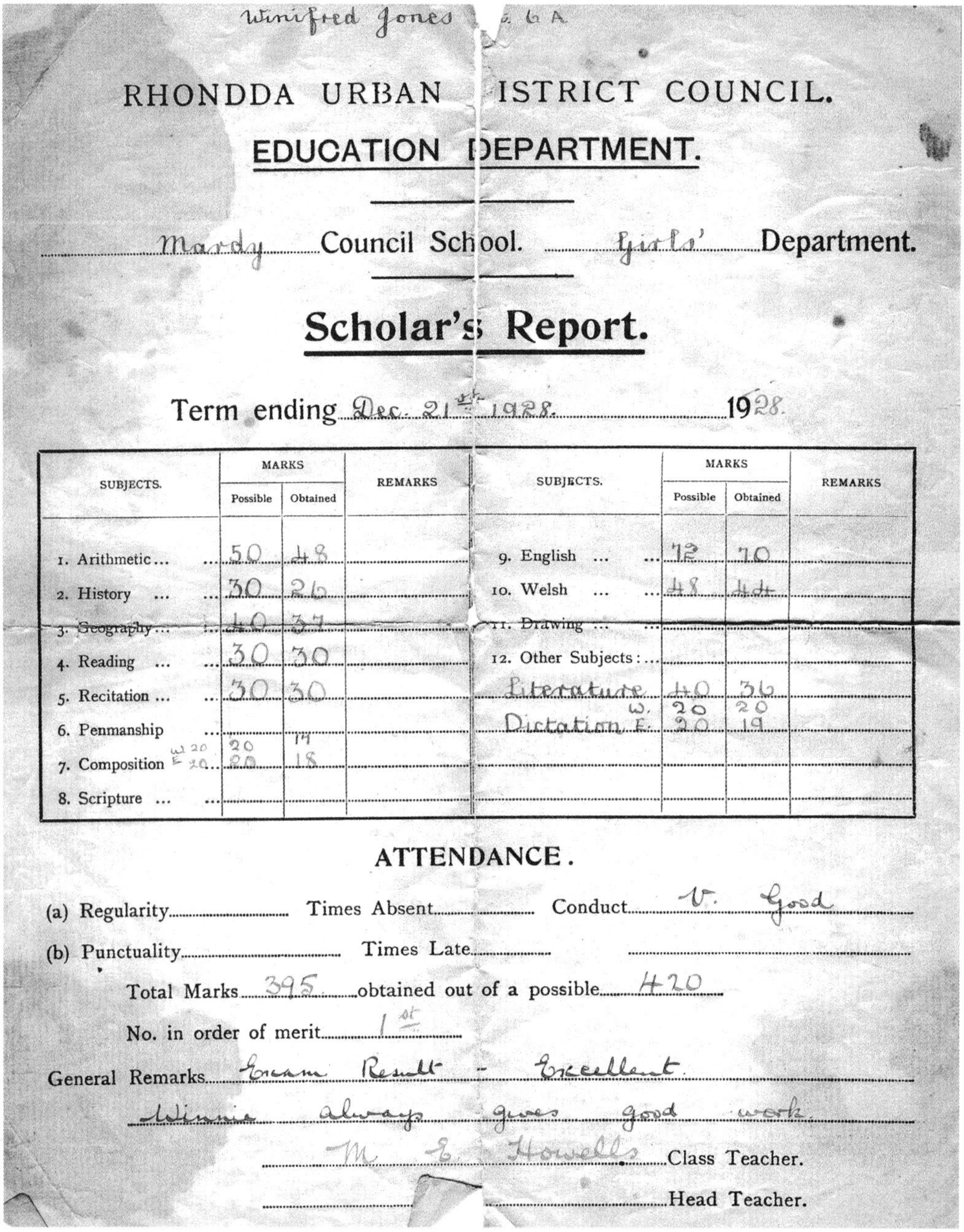

Winifred Jones . 6 A

RHONDDA URBAN DISTRICT COUNCIL.

EDUCATION DEPARTMENT.

Mardy Council School. Girls' Department.

# Scholar's Report.

Term ending Dec. 21st 1928. 1928.

| SUBJECTS. | MARKS Possible | MARKS Obtained | REMARKS | SUBJECTS. | MARKS Possible | MARKS Obtained | REMARKS |
|---|---|---|---|---|---|---|---|
| 1. Arithmetic... | 50 | 48 | | 9. English ... | 72 | 70 | |
| 2. History ... | 30 | 26 | | 10. Welsh ... | 48 | 44 | |
| 3. Geography... | 40 | 37 | | 11. Drawing ... | | | |
| 4. Reading ... | 30 | 30 | | 12. Other Subjects: ... | | | |
| 5. Recitation ... | 30 | 30 | | Literature | 40 | 36 | |
| 6. Penmanship ... | | | | Dictation W. | 20 | 20 | |
| 7. Composition W 20 | 20 | 14 | | Dictation E. | 20 | 19 | |
| 7. Composition E 20 | 20 | 18 | | | | | |
| 8. Scripture ... | | | | | | | |

## ATTENDANCE.

(a) Regularity........ Times Absent........ Conduct V. Good

(b) Punctuality........ Times Late........

Total Marks 395 obtained out of a possible 420

No. in order of merit 1st

General Remarks Exam Result – Excellent.
Winnie always gives good work

M. E. Howells Class Teacher.

........ Head Teacher.

Winifred Jones formerly of North Terrace, Maerdy, Elementary Girls School Report, Class 6a, Term ending 21 December 1928. Courtesy and Etiquette. The root of all good manners is kindness. Good manners are the rules of conduct which boys and girls have drawn up among themselves to make life easier and more pleasant, or to prevent them from doing things that may be harmful. Always be ready to help other people, be bright and cheerful, be clean and tidy, in speaking, and never forget the ordinary words and phrases of courtesy. 'Please' and 'Thank you'.

The Elementary Girls School Standard 3a in 1931. Left to right, back row: Margaret Jones, Morwenna Davies, Thelma Evans, Sylvia Glenys James, Glenys Williams, Sarah Jones, Eunice Evans, Phyllis Jones, Nancy Thomas, Dolly Carter, Joyce Berry. Middle row: Dilys Thomas, May Jones, May Williams, Yvonne James, Agnes Bevan, Peggy Thomas, Tegwen Evans, Gladys Addison, Yvonne Williams, Eira Davies, Odyle Evans. Front row: Miss Catherine Evans (headteacher), Jane Parcel, Betty Lewis, Mary Margaret Thomas, Lucy Beynan, Mary Griffiths, Nancy Day, Megan Davies, Beryl Pring, Joyce Arkless, Miss Elizabeth Mary 'Polly' Hughes (teacher).

The Elementary Girls School Standard 4a in 1931. The photograph includes: Miss Catherine Evans (headteacher), Miss Gwenny 'Check' Morgan (teacher). The Elementary Girls School caretaker was Mrs Jones formerly of Royal Cottages and village milkman Albert Melhuish formerly of Excelsior Terrace delivered the children's one third of a pint of milk to the school.

The Elementary Girls School Standard 5a in 1931. Left to right, back row: Freda Williams, Valmai Davies, Phyllis Jones, Olwen Rees, Glenys Charles, Betty Jones, Peggy Jones, Doreen Berry, Nonnie Pugsley, Peggy Hill, Morfydd Morgan. Middle row: Miss Catherine Evans (headteacher), Eurwen Lewis, Dolly Coleman, Brenda Davies, Thelma Bevan, Edna Tudor, Peggy Jones, Rosa Horner, Vina Williams, Phyllis Fort, Lillian Owen. Front row: Hilda Hopkins, Nancy Webber, Audrey Roberts, Alice Belcher, Verona Corbett, Sally Collins, Moira Davies, Edith Jones, Audrey Evans, Margaret Jones, Miss Esther May Jones (teacher).

The Elementary Girls School Teaching Staff in 1932. Left to right, back row: Miss Doris Llewellyn, Miss Nancy Burgess, Miss Hannah Gadd, Mrs Edith Yarnall, -?-?- , Miss Esther May Jones, Miss Annie Davies, Miss Martha Evans. Front row: Miss Dorothy Jones, Miss Llewella Voyle, Miss Margaret Ann Jones, Miss Catherine Evans (headteacher), Miss Carrie Bamford, Miss Gwenny 'Check' Morgan, Miss Elizabeth Mary 'Polly' Hughes.

The Elementary Girls School in 1933. Left to right, back row: Eirlys Richards, Etta Evans, Gwenith Jones, Sophia Lewis, Glenys Phillips, Phyllis Melhuish, Rhiannon Morris, Ellen -?- , Iris Sully, Doreen Jones, Nancy Davies, Phyllis Davies. Middle Row: Almina Davies, Gladys Greaves, Mavis Screech, Betty Parcel, Miss Martha Evans (teacher), Tonwen Thomas, Dorothy Mary Davies, Hazel Morris, Alma John, Eunice Pugh. Front Row: Doreen -?- , Gwyneth Hughes, Jennie Davies, Ivy May Jones, Olwen Ellis, Elsie James, Olwen Davies, Eirwen Jones, Betty Williams, Iris Jones, Dorothy Davies.

The Elementary Girls School in 1935. Left to right, back row: Iris Sully, Janice Davies, Gwyneth Jones, Rhiannon Morris, Elsie James, Olwen Davies, Betty Parcel. Middle row: Olwen Ellis, Nancy Davies, Dorothy Davies, Dorothy Mary Davies, Etta Evans, Sophie Lewis, Almira Davies, Eirlys Richards. Front row: Eirwen Jones, Betty Williams, Iris Jones. A Western Mail correspondent called Maerdy the 'Oxford of the Rhondda'. Good old Maerdy with its Dramatic Party second to none and its Glee Party with its singing equal to any in the Rhondda.

The Elementary Girls School Teaching Staff in 1935. Left to Right: Miss Gwenny 'Check' Morgan, Miss Martha Evans, Miss Esther May Jones, Miss Annie Davies, -?-?- , Miss Mary Gwyneth Hughes. The entrance exams for students of the Rhondda took place for entrance to the Porth County and Higher Grade Schools. The Maerdy Elementary School students secured the 1st, 2nd, 3rd and 4th places also the 7th, 8th, and the 9th places in the list for all the Rhondda.

The Elementary Girls School full Attendance Pupils Year Ending April 1935. The photograph includes: Nan Duggan, Gwenith Jones, Tegwen Evans, Dilys Thomas, Dilys Humphreys, Dorothy Hadfield, Bernice Jones, Dorothy Davies, Etta Evans, Sophie Lewis, Dorothy Chaffe, Gwyneth Jones, Marion Jones, Betty Barkway, Nora Ninnis, Tegwen Wilshire. In 1935 Maerdy Elementary Girls secured the first four places in the Rhondda Scholarship Examination. Dorothy Mary Davies heads the list, with Eirlys May Richards second and Betty May Williams third

The Elementary Girls School in 1937. The photograph includes: Peggy Jones, Nora Ninnis, Catherine Ellis, Tegwen Davies, Sybil Williams, Arfona Jones. The Girls School hold many happy memories. When the weather was cold, skipping was the game to play, and when it was very cold we would huddle near a place where the coal was kept. If the caretaker was around we ran to the yard, he must have thought we were going to steal the coal to take home! Chasing around the Top Yard was popular, but we got so tired, when we went back into class we felt like having a nap instead of lessons. Jean Williams.

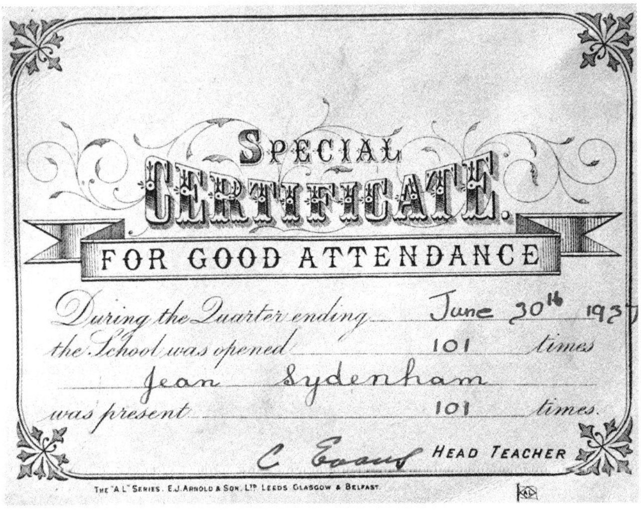

SPECIAL CERTIFICATE
FOR GOOD ATTENDANCE
During the Quarter ending June 30th 1937
the School was opened 101 times
Jean Sydenham
was present 101 times.
C Evans HEAD TEACHER
THE "A.L." SERIES. E.J. ARNOLD & SON, LTD LEEDS GLASGOW & BELFAST.

The Elementary Girls School Special Certificate for Good Attendance awarded to Jean Williams 30 June 1937. Hop Scotch was another game, which meant chalking out squares on the ground to kick the stone – so we waited until we got home to play. As chalk was needed to number each square, at the end of the game we were made to wash all the chalk marks away. Whip and Top was a game mostly played by boys, I wasn't very good at this because I couldn't keep the Top spinning. Jean Williams.

The Elementary Girls School at Rhoose Camp in 1939. The photograph includes: Miss Hannah Gadd (teacher), Nora Jones, Nancy Light, Eirwen Thomas, Brenda Vaughan, Katie Brain, Marion Jones, Margaret Flowers, Denise Holmes, Brenda Davies, Dorothy Charlotte Davies, Deris Evans, Lena Watkins. When I washed the ribbons I used in my hair, I wound them evenly around a bottle filled with warm water. When the ribbons dried they were as new and ready to wear once again.

The Elementary Girls School in 1939. Skipping was a favourite game that we played in the street. The traffic wasn't as busy as it is now. I was always told to change into my 'old shoes' to skip, as it wore your shoes out in no time. When I see children sitting in front of their computers I feel they are missing out on a lot of 'happy hours' and friendly games. I'm glad I spent my time out in the fresh air 'Playing Games' with friends. Jean Williams.

The Elementary Girls School in 1939. In 1935 heartiest congratulations was extended to Miss Nan Duggan, the daughter of Mr and Mrs Trevor Duggan, 32 Richard Street Maerdy, and a pupil of Maerdy Elementary Girls School, who has brought further distinction to Maerdy. At the recent entrance examination to Ferndale secondary and Porth Intermediate Schools.

The Elementary Girls School Teaching Staff in the 1940s. Left to right, back row: Miss Hannah Gadd, Miss Eunice Richards, Miss Gwyneth Hopkins, Miss Annie Davies. Front Row: Miss Nancy Burgess, -?-?- , Mrs Dorothy Jones, Miss Elizabeth Mary 'Polly' Hughes, Miss Mary Gwyneth Hughes. Nan Duggan gained 311 marks out of a possible 350 in each examination, these being the highest marks obtained. Nan has also the distinction of capturing the first prize in Glamorgan at a Scripture Examination held under the auspices of the Welsh Baptist Union.

Right: Edith Avril Berry and Patricia Mary Berry Pupils at the Elementary Girls School in 1941. In 1935 pupils of the Maerdy Elementary Schools gained the following places: 2nd, 4th, 5th, 6th, 8th, 9th, 10th, 11th, 17th, etc a truly great achievement. We congratulate the entire staff of the Maerdy schools. We extend heartiest congratulations to the pupils of the Maerdy Elementary Girls School on their remarkable successes in the special examinations for the children between the ages of 13 and 14 years for the entrance to Form 3 of either the new Ferndale Secondary School or the Porth Intermediate School. Maerdy pupils sat the examinations and the following were successful: Iris Ruby Hughes, 93 Maerdy Road; Mavis Screech, 23 Wood Street; Gladys Williams, James Street.

Left: The Parkinson's Scholar's Guide from the 1940s. A page for girls. Every girl desires to be a help to her mother, and one of the best means of helping is by mending, and even making her own clothes, or, at least, some of them. Begin by making simple underwear, and, as skill in sewing is acquired, more ambitious garments may be attempted. Embroidery, also, may be attempted, and this need not be confined to clothes, but may be used on covers and cushions etc., for the home. For older girls, there are various handicrafts which will be found to give great enjoyment, besides being eminently practical or ornamental. Amongst these are: glove-making, leather work, hand-loom weaving, basket-making, etc. Knitting and crocheting may also be attempted, and many useful and beautiful things can be made by these methods. Remember that it is very often the people who are busiest who are the happiest.

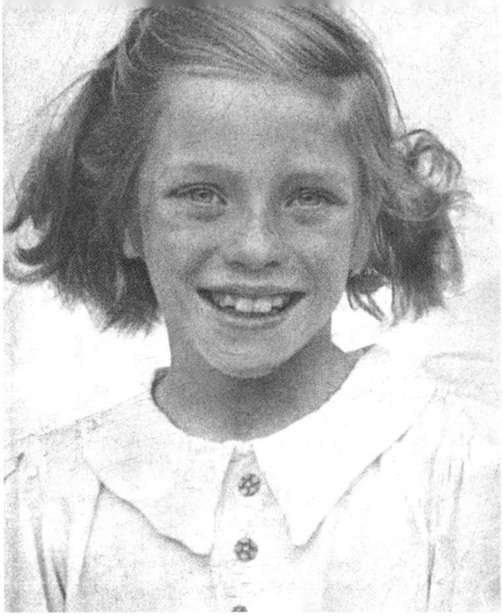

Left: Rose Cripps Pupil at the Elementary Girls School in 1941. Right: Eirona James Pupil at the Elementary Girls School in 1944. We were taught to take care of our books in school. They were kept in a dry room, in a large book case. When we opened a new book we had clean hands and we laid it on a clean table and took care when turning the pages.

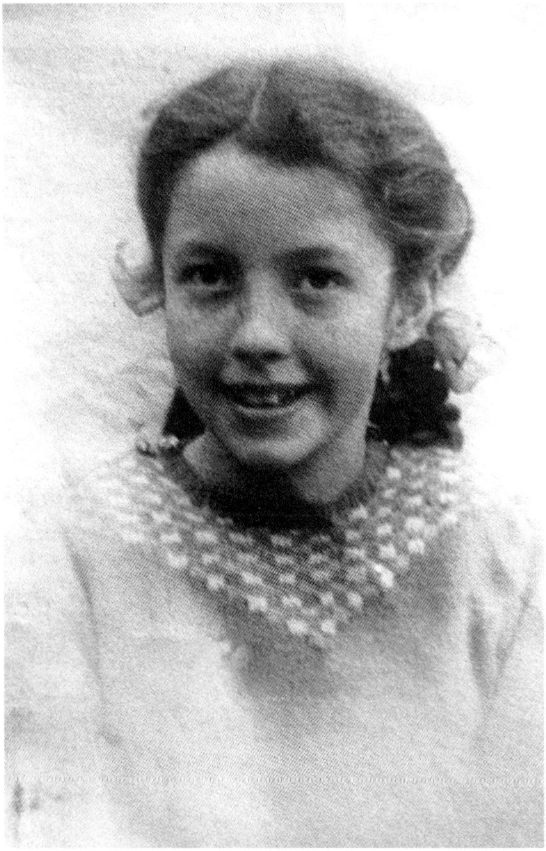

Left: Lyneth Rees Pupil at the Elementary Girls School in 1945. We were taught Welsh at school from a book called Bi Lingual Readers, Primer Part 1. Y Llyfr Cyntaf I'r Plant Bach. The Hughes & Son's educational series for students and school use had a grammar of the Welsh Language, Welsh Exercises, Welsh Synonyms, English-Welsh and Welsh-English Dictionary. The price of the book was 4d (approximately 2p).

When school lessons were over the children joyfully headed for the park to play. Maerdy Park was opened by Dr Glanville Morris in May 1916; it is situated at the top end of Maerdy village and has always been a popular place for children to enjoy themselves on the roundabout and swings. In 1935 the play area consisted of a roundabout, swings, slide, and a Japanese push. There was an enclosed 'Kick about Area' as far as the No. 1 and No. 2 Colliery boundary. A narrow path separated the park and the colliery ground which led to 'Jubilee Walk'.

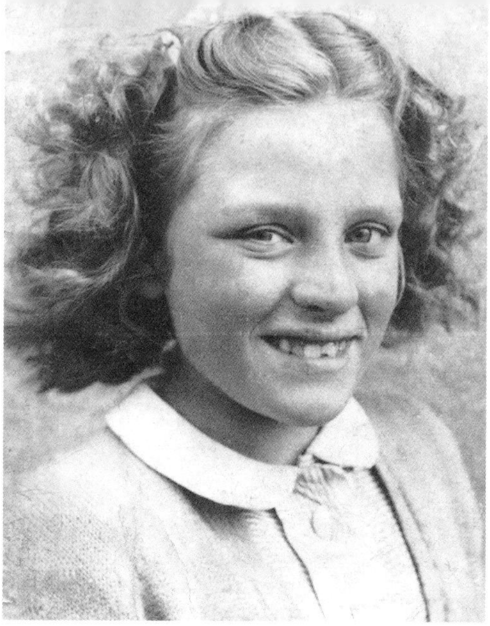

Left: Ruth Griffiths Pupil at the Elementary Girls School in 1945. Right: Audrey Cripps Pupil at the Elementary Girls School in 1947. Throughout the years the schools at Maerdy have used Bethania Vestry, Seion Vestry, Ebenezer Vestry (now Teify House) and Maerdy Workmen's Hall for lessons, school concerts and festive plays.

The Elementary Girls School in the 1940s. The Photograph includes: Dorothy Hadfield, Mary Jones, Mary Cox. When we were in school we often stained our clothes when we filled the ink wells with black ink. These stains were removed by using lemon juice or milk. When all the stain had been removed we would steep the clothing in cold water all night before washing it and when we fell down while playing in the school yard we would soak the blood stained clothing in cold salt water over night.

The Elementary School Monday 24 May 1948. Fire broke out at the school in the early hours of Monday morning 24 May 1948, completely destroying the school, all was lost. Maerdy Elementary School was opened on Monday 6 September 1880. The school had mixed classes. In 1889 the school had separate facilities for boys and girls, the girls using the lower or Ferndale end of the building. In those days boys and girls were never allowed to mix even at playtimes as there was a wall separating the playgrounds. The front railings of the school can still be seen, as the site was sadly never developed for any other purpose. The pupils were sent to Ferndale Junior 'lower' School, Ferndale Duffryn Girls and Infant Schools, Ferndale Boys and Infants Schools, Blaenllechau Infant School and Maerdy Infant School. Transport was arranges with the Rhondda Transport Company for buses to transport the children to and from Maerdy at a cost of £8 per day. The new Junior School built in 1952 with mixed classes is light and modern with a large assembly hall, a gymnasium and indoor toilets, something many children did not have at home in 1952. Arwyn Williams.

The fire grates used to be so full of coal giving out so much warmth and making the homes so comfortable and cheerful for everybody, especially the children playing on the hearthstone, and nothing but their laughter and singing to be heard until they went to their little beds to rest with an absurd patriotic pride they feel that there is no place on God's earth to be compared with the Rhondda and no people to be compared with the people of the Rhondda. Maerdy was called the Musical Village, every house had some musical instruments mostly pianos. The school children sang in choirs and the singing was a pleasure to the ear. Maerdy was a prosperous and happy village.

The children of the Maerdy Schools have always been on the top of the lists, and it is a great consolation they don't forget the little village where they were born and reared up and received their education thus making them an asset in this world of ours and they are always glad to come back to see Maerdy now and again when they have a chance, for nothing beats the mountain air to restore the colour to their cheeks and back to good health. Maerdy is known as the healthiest place in the Valley and one Doctor has said years ago "A good ride on top of the tram up to the top of Maerdy was as good as a dose of medicine and better, and to walk over its mountains was better still", and all those that go away from here and come back again say that there is no water like ours for quenching the thirst and the first thing they do is to have a glass of Maerdy water. Anthony Lewis.

## Maerdy School Days

*Today, I came, I saw, I spoke.*
*With friends of yesteryear.*
*Of wondrous days long long ago.*
*And memories sincere.*

*We remembered and laughed as words*
*Of song flowed free as wine,*
*For time stood still when we all met,*
*Then it was time to dine.*

*I remembered with great "hiraeth",*
*A Welsh School, classroom too,*
*Mental Arithmetic – A Story,*
*As we sat – two by two.*

*A teacher young and lovely,*
*Miss Evans was her name,*
*Strict and firm in teaching,*
*But we loved her just the same.*

*These were good days, and tears fell,*
*Hard work and days of fun,*
*Throughout those Maerdy School Days,*
*Our respect, Miss. Evans won.*

*Then the bell, and school was over,*
*A new world lay ahead,*
*'Till that night, an invitation,*
*A 'Reunion' you both said.*

*Our friendship I shall cherish,*
*Fifty years with memories too,*
*A big 'thank you' to you both,*
*Good Health and God Bless You.*

*Betty Parcel Age 77 formerly of Griffith Street*

## School Days Revisited

*We felt so proud, long, long ago,*
*Walking through the girls' school doors,*
*Miss Phillips was our governess,*
*Classrooms were neat, there was no mess.*

*Standard one was really great,*
*History, geography, dinners on a plate,*
*Welsh, PT Rounders too,*
*Scripture, Knitting, Sewing to do.*

*There was a concert I recall,*
*It was held in Maerdy Hall,*
*We sang and danced, figure marched too,*
*The tunes were famous in World War Two.*

*Numbers rose and classes grew,*
*Miss Gadd taught Knitting in Bethania pews,*
*The boys' school found it just the same,*
*In Seion vestry they had games.*

*Being a monitor was a thrill,*
*Giving out and collecting was the drill,*
*Clearing paint and mixing ink,*
*We did it all in a wink.*

*But the best job of all*
*Was ringing the hand bell by the school wall.*

*Lyneth Bevan Age 66 of Station Terrace*
*A recycled Maerdy School Days teenager*

# *Three*
# The Junior School

To write the history of this school must be one of the hardest things I have been asked to write. The school, any school, cannot stand on its own – everything that happens in the village impinges on school, so you cannot comment on school and education without relating to local events – and this would take a book on its own.

Maerdy Junior School opened on 12 May 1952. To quote from the log – book (the Headteacher at that time was Eddie Parry, B.Sc.)

"This new school was opened today and 291 children were admitted having been transferred from Ferndale Junior Mixed and Maerdy Infants Schools ….. (I) found that all pupils had settled in very smoothly".

This was followed by the official opening on 30 June by Councillor M. Harcombe – the official plaque can be seen in the foyer.

Throughout its 50 year history the school has seen great successes and fortunately to a far lesser extent, great tragedies when accidents or sudden death have had traumatic effects on both staff and children. Our successes can be seen every day when you look at the people of Maerdy who attended this school in their youth. To have achieved an ambition in life gives a great lift, whether it be academic, sporting, performing or just pure job satisfaction. Many of the foundations were laid in this school by often dedicated teachers, and children who have the Welsh desire and ability to learn. So many of our pupils have gone on through secondary education to make their mark in the world.

Maerdy Junior School has always been held in high regard in the field of education. This is even more true today where, through our information communication technology we lead the country. School has changed (we now have less than 150 pupils), but the children remain the same. They all come to school carrying with them problems, successes and dreams. Your school, Maerdy Junior School, continues to strive to address them all. We hope you are as proud of us as we are of you and the village of Maerdy.

Maerdy Junior School and the community live hand in hand. The successes of one are reflected in the successes of the other. It is a partnership with the strongest of links, and long may it be so.

Mr Peter Blake Junior School Headteacher

The Junior School during construction in 1952. Since the school began the staff, children, governors, parents and the local people of the village have raised thousands of pounds to benefit the school and the children in their education. Thanks must be given to one and all that have given their time and help in any way, little or large, over the past fifty years. There is a small account in the following chapter of some achievements and money raised for the school.

## The junior school headteachers from 1952 to date

| | | |
|---|---|---|
| 1952 | 1955 | Mr Edward Parry |
| 1955 | 1965 | Mr Llewellyn Jarman |
| 1965 | 1968 | Mr Thomas Daniels |
| 1968 | 1973 | Mr Emrys Davies |
| 1973 | 1984 | Mr John Aeron Lewis |
| 1984 | 1988 | Mr Wynford Evans |
| 1988 | 1995 | Mrs Patricia Davies |
| 1995 | (to date) | Mr Peter Blake |

**Life is a long time!**

1952. Maerdy Junior School opened; my father was the first teacher here and my sister was a pupil.
1954. I came here as a boy.
1957. My future wife started in standard 1.
1971. I returned as a teacher.
1974. I saw my daughter enrolled.
1995. I achieved a great professional ambition and became Headteacher.
2001. I saw my first grand daughter start in Year 3 and I can't wait for the second!
50 years old this year - not me! - the school.
30 years of my life.
50 years of my family history.
50 years at Maerdy Junior School.

Mr Peter Blake Headteacher

The Junior School Completed in 1952. It cost £95,000 to build. The following words hang on the wall in the school Assembly Hall for everyone to see. Do all the good you can. By all the means you can. In all the ways you can. In all the places you can. At all the times you can. To all the people that you can. As long as ever you can.

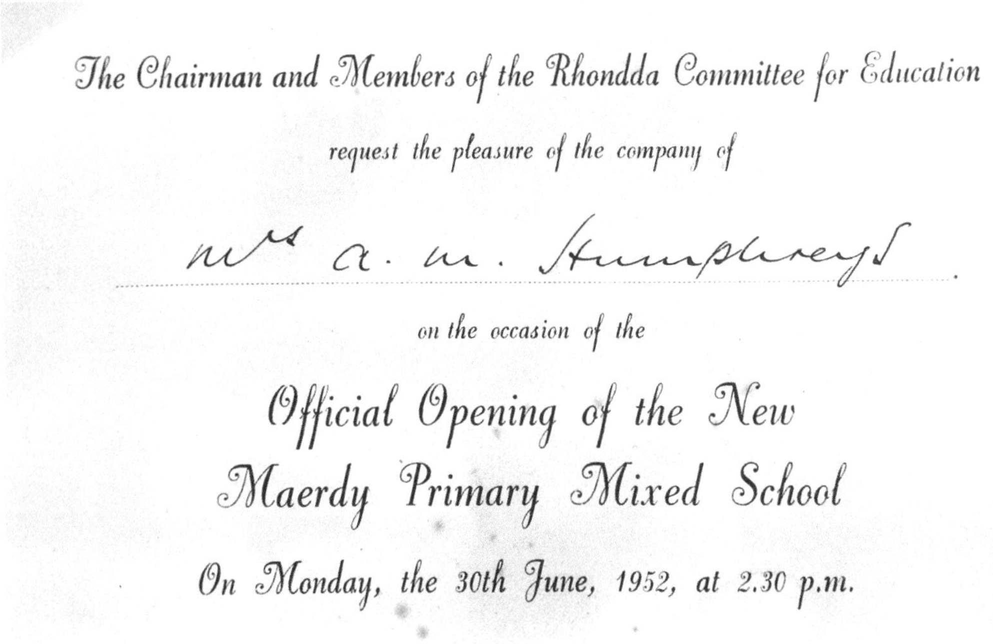

The Chairman and Members of the Rhondda Committee for Education

request the pleasure of the company of

Mrs A. M. Humphreys

on the occasion of the

Official Opening of the New

Maerdy Primary Mixed School

On Monday, the 30th June, 1952, at 2.30 p.m.

Maerdy Junior School was officially opened at 2:30p.m. on Monday 30 June 1952. My School. Maths everyday, Yelling at playtime, Spelling tests, Chips, cake and custard in the canteen, Homework (horrible), Once a week we have certificates in Assembly, Outside Mr Blake's room if you're naughty, Lots of lovely teachers. Jessica Richards Year 3 Age 7.

The Junior School in 1952. Left to right, back row: Wynford Davies, Leslie Thomas, Glanville Belcher, Alan Taylor, Michael Cavacuiti, Terry Smith, Trevor Morgan, Michael Rogers, Bryan Davies, Mervyn Griffiths, Lyndon Rees. Middle row: Mr Edward Parry (headteacher), Bryan Morris, David Bowyer, Keith Evans, Christine Llewellyn, Linda Middleton, John Griffiths, Terry Griffiths, Russell Smith, Mr Baden Adams (teacher). Front row: Mair Roberts, Evana Lewis, Marilyn Jones, Margaret Cripps, Janice Evans, Christine Cooper, Anne Smith, Anne Whitehead, Gwenda Tibbles, Pearl Miller, Pamela Edwards.

The Junior School in 1952. The photograph includes: Mr Edward Parry (headteacher), Malcolm Evans, Billy Richards, Ian Brown, Barry Jones, Anthony Wharton, Kenneth Greaves, Hayden Jones, Victor Hooper, Front row: Mavis Hughes, Valerie Rees, Maureen Morris, Carol Everson, Norma Roberts, Margaret Jones, Sheila Jones, Pauline Jones, Valmai Rosser, Kathleen Evans, Diane Newton, Valerie Davies, Mr Vincent Evans (teacher).

The Junior School Standard 2 in 1953. Left to right, back row: Mr Edward Parry (headteacher), Dennis Lewis, Royston Jones, Ronald Gill, Billy Hayes, John McGeogh, Raymond Basset, Graham Evans, Bernard Williams, Raymond Hopkins, David George Lewis, -?-?- , Raymond Lovell, Jeffrey Piper, Mrs Hilda Bateson (teacher). Front Row: Ken Griffiths, Carol Jones, Pauline -?- , Sheila Evans, Marilyn Evans, Ann Loveday, Linda Griffiths, Marilyn Farmer, Iris Pugh, John Lawless.

The Junior School in 1953. The photograph includes: Thelma Jones, Meryl Evans, Bernard Williams, Raymond Hopkins, Carole Marden, Tony Comey, Raymond Lovell, Ken Griffiths, Denver Vaughan, Ann Loveday, Marilyn Farmer, Mrs Margaret Edwards (teacher), Keith Rowlands, Iris Pugh, Joan Vaughan, Graham Evans, Jeffrey Piper, Billy Hayes, Dennis Lewis, Linda Griffiths, Raymond Basset, Royston Jones, Victor Parry.

Junior School Pupils Kay Davies and Margaret Jones playing 'Shop' in the school grounds in 1954. On the side of a hill with a lovely view, Stands our school, all shiny and new, With teachers and pupils so healthy and hardy, The school that I mean is the primary Maerdy. Beryl Victoreen Edmunds Age 82 of Glanville Terrace.

The Junior School Standard 1a June 1955. Left to right, back row: Lyn Morris, Brian Jones, John Wiltshire, Susan Wharton, Lynne Jones, Miss Elizabeth Mary 'Polly' Hughes (teacher). Third row: Stephen Tilling, Michael Evans, Carol Francis, Sandra Davies, Teresa Edgell, Joan Davies, Gaynor Jones. Second row: Stuart Davies, Alan Williams, David Jones, Pauline Thomas, Elisabeth Parry, Susan Smith, Margaret Turner, Eironwy Evans. Front row: Royston Pudsey, Russell Chamberlain, Carl Haines, Trevor John, Gillian Davies, Janice Venning.

The Junior School in 1955. Left to right back row: Mr Harold Blake (teacher), Leslie Thomas, Ceri Thomas, John Lawless, Ronald Gill, Basil Rees, Malcolm Thomas, John McGeogh, Kenneth Williams, Alan Evans, Arthur Lewis, Clive Jones. Middle row: John Michael Jones, Garfield Growther, Sheila Osborne, Gaynor Davies, Myra Llewellyn, Pauline Jones, Kay Davies, Valerie Davies, Larraine 'Sis' Rogers, Sonia Roberts, Denver Vaughan, Brian Evans. Front row: Janet Voyle, Pauline -?- , Donna Stevens, Margaret Jones, Gaynor Smith, Marilyn Sims, Mavis Hughes, Sheila Gabriel, Andrea Phillips, Meryl Evans.

The Junior School in 1956. The photograph includes: Jeff Lewis, Alan Hunt, John Voyle, Lorna Davies, Hillary Evans, Wayne Gabriel, Angela Williams, Patricia Thomas, Carol Davies, Heather Jones, Hillary Thomas, Miss Irene Thomas (teacher). Over the past years the school has entertained hundreds of people with very successful concerts and sporting events.

The Junior School Athletic Team in 1957. The photograph includes: Mr Harold Blake (sports teacher), Ronald Payne, David Dunham, Harry Parry, Byron Manning, Ken Griffiths, David Lewis, John Lawless, John Voyle, Raymond Evans, John Roberts, Michael Sweet, Mr Llewellyn Jarman (headteacher). Congratulations to the team and school pupils for their dedication and training practice.

The Junior School Standard 3 April 1957. Left to right, back row: Colin Evans, Malcolm Poole, Lesley Vincent, John Satherly, John Richards, Gerald Evans, Steven Sims. Third row: Mr Llewellyn Jarman (headteacher), Brian Jordan, Alan Corcoran, Michael Blaney, Leslie Lovell, Leslie Hunt, Michael Richards, Terry Goodwin, David Dunham, Derek Parry, Alan Harvey, Mrs Dorothy Jones (teacher). Second row: Frances Ball, Hilary Thomas, Maureen Gregory, Maureen Richards, Dwynwen Thomas, Avril Tann, Marilyn Bevan. Front row: Cynthia Evans, Patricia Light, Ann Jones.

The Junior School XI Football League Champions 1957/58 season. Left to right, back row: Mr Harold Blake (teacher), Mr William John Griffiths (teacher), Mr Llewellyn Jarman (headteacher). Middle row: David Vaughan, Ray Evans, Michael Wharton, Eddie Murray, Dennis Lark, Michael Vincent, John Roberts. Front row: Byron Manning, Lyn Jones, Brian Knight, Ken Davies, David Gwilym Jones. Congratulations to the team and school pupils for their dedication and training practice.

The Junior School Saint David's Day 1 March 1958. My School. My school is the best school I have been to. None of the teachers are grumpy. They treat us all the same. Mr Blake is so very kind he is our headteacher. I have only been in this school for two years, It has been great, I'm glad I'm here for another two years. Bernadette Wood Year 4 Age 8.

The Junior School Standard 1a 1959. The photograph includes: Keith Gregory, Gareth Jones, Kenneth Roberts, Sammy Ward, Kerry Williams, John Thomas, Jimmy Hall, Brian Davies, David Mullins, Paul Williams, Howard Thomas, Gloria Dixon, Elwyn Cox, Alan Williams, Marion Jones, Susan Davies, Joanne Chaffe, Susan Griffiths, Jean Thomas, Kay Harvey, Christine Hayes, Ann Fitzgerald, Elizabeth Marden, Christine Greenslade, Tommy Mullins, Beverly Coombes.

Left: Play Time at the Junior School in 1959. Left to right: Jimmy Hall, Gareth Jones, Sammy Ward. Our School. The Maerdy Junior School stands firm and strong, Its walls have heard so many songs. Each generation that's passed through remembers their school days with memories still new. The sports day the parties the lessons we learned, the teachers with patience who have helped us through. One day when we are older we will look back and say, our school days were happy and hopefully made the very proud adults we are today. Sean Warren Year 5 Age 10.

Playing Football in the Schoolyard in 1960. The photograph includes: Byron James, Howard Thomas, Alan Williams, Sammy Ward, Ken Roberts, Robert Lewis. My School. I really like my school, The teachers are really cool. I like to play in the yard, But it hasn't got a pool. My favourite lesson is Welsh, In Welsh, we have lots of fun. I also like the subject: Maths, We count to three hundred and one. Matthew Davies Year 3 Age 7.

The Junior School Concert in 1960. The photograph includes: Pat Morgan, Helen Rowe, Glyn Edmunds, Graham Edwards, Melvyn Davies, Alan Jones, June Pudsey, June Morgan, Mair Mortimer, Cynthia John, Lynn Howells, Gareth Mortimer, Edward Kapps, Phillip Williams, Geoffrey Hamer, Eirlys Jones, Paul Davies, Moira Thomas, Jennifer Jenkins, Joyce Weston Thomas, Celia Lewis, Yvonne Jones, Sheila Smith.

The Junior School Saint David's Day 1 March 1961. The photograph includes: J. Allen, C. Greenslade, S. Griffiths, J. Chaffe, S. Davies, M. Jones, G. Razey, H. Osbourne, L. Jenkins, M. Davies, J. Thomas, S. Lloyd, G. Dixon, B. Thomas, C. Rich, A. Llewellyn, A. Razey, A. Thomas, J. John, M. Parry, G. Parcel, L. Jones, E. Davies, A. Hughes, B. Tucker, J. Thomas, C. Thomas, M. Hopkins, L. Loveday, C. Lewis, M. Gabriel, M. Thomas, P. Thomas, S. Smith, J. Thomas, Y. Jones, E. Jones, C. Newt, I. Richardson, S. Woodhouse, S. Palmer, M. Jones.

The Junior School in 1961. Left to right, back row: Mr William John Griffiths (teacher) R. Perry, S. Albertelli, J.R. Davies, K. Davies, S. Davies, A. Edwards, R. Williams, L. Ketherey, Mr Llewellyn Jarman (headteacher). Third row: G. Evans, P. Jones, R. Howells, S. Lloyd, W. Howells, K. Lewis, S. Knight, G. Razey, G. Richardson, F. Edgell, A. Bowen. Second row: A. Llewellyn, C. Jones, T. Lloyd, M. Withers, B. Coombes, O. Jones, H. Davies, B. Mazey, F. Williams. Front row: G. L'Homme, -?-?- , Colin -?- , K. Jones.

The Junior School in 1962. Left to right, back row: M. Jarrat, A. Ronka, M. Watkins, J. Jones, G. Beach, W. Jones, W. Modrate, M. Jones. Third row: Mrs Dorothy Jones (teacher), C. Jones, C. Casey, A. Bevan, A. Phillips, E. Cox, L. Jones, S. Parry, H. Lovell, A. John, Mr Llewellyn Jarman (headteacher). Second row: I. Evans, I. Jones, C. Clements, A. Williams, J. Lewis, L. Jones. J. Voyle. L. Jones. S. Jarrat. Front row: G. Dutson, R. Mullin, G. Kibble, F. Rossiter.

The Junior School in 1962. Left to right, back row: Mr Llewellyn Jarman (headteacher), John Miles, Thomas Stephan Neville, Malcolm Roberts, M. Burridge, Kelvin Davies, Meurig Lewis, Emrys Morgan. Third Row: Royston Gauvain, Melvin Stinchcombe, John Thomas, Robert Davies, Alan Saunders, Nigel Best, Peter Fortt, David Jones, Ian Wells, Mrs Aileen John (teacher). Second Row: Tina Dean, Myra Davies, Elaine Buxton, Pauline Evans, Linda Hughes, Wendy Radcliff, Eirwen Williams, Pauline Day, Jackie Clements. Front Row: Gareth Jones, Linda Miles, Nerissa Richards, David Bevan.

The Junior School Standard 4a Saint David's Day 1 March 1963. With drifts of snow in the school yard. The photograph includes: Margaret Parry, Ann Razey, Christie Greenslade, Jean Thomas, Kay Harvey, Ann Hughes, Susan Davies, Marion Jones, Susan Griffiths.

The Junior School in 1963. Left to right, Back row: Mr Harold Blake (sports teacher), John Thomas, Alan Williams, Jimmy Hall, Hazel Osborne, Gloria Dixon, David Evans, Keith Gregory, Kenneth Roberts, Mr Llewellyn Jarman (headteacher). Third row: Ann Razey, Susan Davies, Marian Jones, Helen Jones, Ann Hughes, Christine Greenslade, Christine Hayes, Beryl Thomas, Janice Williams. Second row: Lynn Jenkins, Susan Griffiths, Barbara Pudsey, Jean Thomas, Margaret Parry, Elizabeth Marden, Ann Fitzgerald, Kay Harvey, Norma Davies, Carol L'Homme, Front Row: Colin Everson, Sammy Ward, Gareth Jones.

The Junior School Football Team in 1963. The photograph includes: Michael Davies, David Thomas, Robert L'Homme, Keith Jones, Ronnie Lewis, Gareth Griffiths, Martyn Davies, Gary Edwards, Ronnie Williams, Gareth Jones. Pupils move onto the Community School to attain both academic and sporting honours.

The Junior School Sports Team in 1963. The photograph includes: Mrs Irene Jones (teacher), Mr Llewellyn Jarman (headteacher), Mr Harold Blake (sports teacher), D. Pugh, F. Edgell, M. Ball, K. Roberts, P. Williams, C. Everson, D. Evans, H. Thomas, K. Gregory, S. Albertelli, L. Young, G. Dixon, B. Coombes, C. Howe, E. Marden, G. Razey, M. Parry, M. Jones, J. Thomas, A. Fitzgerald, A. Razey, J. Chaffe, R. Ward, A. Evans, G. Evans, K. Davies, M. Roberts, R. L'Homme, N. Light, D. Thomas, M. Cavaciuti, B. Davies, N. Roberts, P. Williams, A. Jones, V. Tann, C. Jones, J. Evans.

The Junior School in 1964. Left to right, back row: Mr Llewellyn Jarman (headteacher), G. Jones, D. Thomas, R. Davies, R. Jones, -?- Jenkins, M. Davies, P. Vandor. Third row: D. Sydenham, R. Williams, R. L'Homme, R. Williams, J. Francis, D. Kapps, R. Carey, D. Hopkins, Neil -?- , K. Gummer, A. Gwilym, Mrs Dorothy Jones (teacher). Second row: G. Davies, P. Gifford, G. Thomas, A. Lewis, J. Evans, P.A. Thomas, L. Jones, K. Lewis, P. Knight. Front row: S. Murray, N. Seldon, L. Jones, C. Williams, G. Cavell, E. Petherick, P. Mazey, P. Thomas, J. Harvey.

The Junior School in 1965. Fire broke out at Maerdy infant school on 18 November 1964. Two classes were accommodated at the Junior School and the remainder at Ebenezer vestry. Left to right, back row: Mrs Veronica Jarman (teacher), K. Evans, N. Evans, T. Vaughan, ? Jones, A. Smith, K. Hanley, P. Steel. Third row: S. Parmie, G. Griffiths, J. Williams, J. Roberts, M. Lewis, -?-?- , W. Marsh, R. Pike, P. Buxton, C. Lawless. Second Row: J. Crotty, A. Thomas, E. Evans, J. Withers, E. Dingle, D. Cooper, V. Jones, S. Cooling, R. Pugh. Front row: G. Pride, E. Williams, A. Mathews, M. Davies, M. Lewis.

The Junior School Sports Team in 1965. The photograph includes: Peter Fortt, Malcolm Roberts, Anthony Evans, Ronald Ward, Steve Rossiter, Kelvin Daniel, David Thomas, John Gregory, Jeff Palmer, Gareth Griffiths, Steven Daniel, Steven Albertelli, Jeff Watkins, Michael Davies, Jane Parker, Nerisa Richards, Janice Evans, Andrea Thomas, Avril Jones, Christine Williams, Coleen Jones, Shirley Lovell, Kathleen Melhuish, Elaine Howells, Elaine L'Homme, Annette Pride, Mrs Irene Jones (teacher), Mr. Llewellyn Jarman (headteacher), Mr Harold Blake (sports teacher).

The Junior School in 1965. The photograph includes: Mrs Tessa Evans (teacher), Mrs Dorothy Jones (teacher), Jane Parker, Pauline Williams, Avril Jones, Linda Davies, Susan Stanway. Pupils have sung before the Bishop of Llandaff, have been on radio from Glyncornel Environment Centre, sung on Songs of Praise and have been a centre page article in the Western Mail for the school computer provision.

The Junior School Teaching Staff in 1965. Left to right, back row: Miss Fay Palmer (school secretary), Mrs Eunice McNamara, Mrs Aileen John, Mr Maelgwyn Jones, Mr Harold Blake, Mr Alan Trottman, Mrs Dorothy Jones, Mrs Tessa Evans, Mrs Mair Francis. Front row: Mrs Irene Jones, Mr Vincent Evans, Mr Llewellyn Jarman (headteacher), Miss Elizabeth Mary 'Polly' Hughes, Mrs Elizabeth Phillips.

The Junior School in 1965. The photograph includes: Mr Llewellyn Jarman (headteacher), Gareth Griffiths, Wynford Evans, Michael Davies, John 'Deo' Davies, Keith Jones, Stephen Davies, Mrs Elizabeth Phillips (teacher), Stuart Fry, Sandra Thomas, Dawn Farmer, Shirley Lovell, Janice Williams, Llinos Thomas, Rita Crotty, Lynette Saunders, Karen Minton, Karen Jones, Helen Pike, Mair Huggins, Vanessa Tann, Julie Herbert, June Ballinger.

The Junior School in 1965. Left to right, back row: Peter Havard, Geoffrey Palmer, Anthony Evans, Curtis Morgan, Robert Kettlety, Gerwyn Evans, Adrian Jones. Third row: Mrs Tessa Evans (teacher), Russell -?- (student teacher), Lorraine Wyatt, Jane Parker, Jean Davies, Bethan Williams, Susan Stanway, Linda Davies, Pauline Williams, Avril Jones, Olwen Owens, Dallas Robert, Mr Llewellyn Jarman (headteacher). Second row: Maria Cavaciuti, Christina Davies, Patricia Herbert, Andrea Thomas, Janice Phillips, Patricia Hamer, Dilys Jones, Maria Fedyck, Coleen Jones. Front row: John Vandor, Gary Lord, Kerry Steele, Ronald Ward, David Gummer, Colin Jones.

The Junior School Football League Champions and Cup Winners 1965/1966 season. Left to right, back row: Mr Thomas Daniels (headteacher), Mr Maelgwyn Jones (teacher), Mr Harold Blake (sports teacher), Mr Haydn Jones (teacher). Third row: Byron Parry, Gareth Griffiths, Gary Edwards, Ronnie Williams, David Gwilym. Second row: Richard Davies, David Thomas, Robert L'Homme, Gareth Jones, Richard Jones. Front row: Martin Davies, Michael Davies, Keith Jones, Robert Williams, Ronnie Lewis.

Left: David Thomas being presented with his Junior School Football League Champions and Cup Winners Badge, 1965/1966 season by Deputy Mayor Mr Warren Morgan. The school has won overall 17 out of the last 26 annual sports meetings, produced CD ROMs involving the Teacher Training Agency, RCT Sharing Good Practice, SouthWales Fire Service and the Welsh Arts Council, raised money for Red Nose Day, Tŷ Hafan the Children's Hospice in Wales, Operation Christmas Child and raised over £1,000 for Cancer Research Cymru by abseiling down a Cardiff Hotel. But most important the school celebrates success daily!

The Juniors School Rhondda Fach Cup Winners 1966/1967 season. Left to right, back row: Alan Evans, Dayne Jones, Tommy Vandor, Jeffrey Palmer, Dennis Rossiter, Gareth 'Chippo' Griffiths, Colin Lewis. Front row: Wayne Rosser, Robert Evans, Michael Davies (captain), Ronnie Lewis, Byron Parry.

The Junior School in 1966. The photograph includes: Ray Seldon, Kay Jones. Pupils have sung in public with our friends from Teify House, and held a high reputation for music, they have compiled a museum guide for the national Museum; calendars were made and printed for the Millennium and the school has won a sculpture competition.

The Junior School in 1967. The photograph includes: Mr Thomas Daniels (headteacher), Mrs Mair Francis (teacher), Michael Gregory, Malcolm Gregory, Cheryl Hadfield, Kevin Richard, Mick Jones, John Owens, Allen Hughes, Sharon Rees, Steven Williams, Julie Simmons, Diane Evans, Ann Jones, Wendy Thomas, Siân Lock, Julie Harris, Anthony Gallagher, Diane Villis.

The Junior School in 1968. Left to right, back row: Mrs Veronica Harper (teacher), Robert Lewis, John Davies, Jeffrey Roberts, Neil Griffiths, Alan Hunt, Mr Thomas Daniels (headteacher). Third row: Paul Lewis, Christopher -?- , Alan Rogers, John Crotty, Raymond Harris, Keith Hanley, Stephen L'Homme, Vivian Thomas. Second row: Beverly Razey, Vanessa Coles, Julie Herbert, Susan Thomas, Lynne Francis, Annette Francis, Leslie Woods, Diane Maddox, Linda Murray, Diane Petherick. Front row: Edith Williams, Gillian Pride, Angela Hunt, Pamela Edwards, Eleanor Evans.

The Junior School in 1968. Left to right, back row: Mrs Dorothy Jones (teacher), Gareth Thomas, Brian Thomas, Michael Davies, Anthony Evans, Alan Holland, Anthony Gaspar, Mark Jenkins, Mr Thomas Daniels (headteacher). Third row: David Parry, Ralph Marden, Alan Evans, Julie Harris, Ceri Thomas, Heather Roberts, Beverly Tennant, Nicholas Jones, Philip McNamara, Stephen Jones. Second row: Elaine Harrison, Patricia Evans, Lorna Alcock, Meryl Thomas, Susan Oliver, Alison Thomas, Debbie Hill, Noreen Smith, Avril Davies, Katy Thomas, Helen Lewis. Front row: Janet Jones, Christine Hickman, Debra Earland, Wendy Vincent, Dawn Podmore.

The Junior School Teaching Staff in 1968. Left to Right: Miss Susan Davies, Mrs Ann Scofield, Mrs Mair Francis, Mrs Aileen John, Mr Hayden Jones, Mrs Veronica Harper, Mr Thomas Daniels (headteacher), Mr Harold Blake, Mrs Glenys Gwynne, Mr Vincent Evans, Mrs Irene Jones, Mr Maelgwyn Jones, Mrs Dorothy Jones.

The Junior School Concert at Bethania Chapel in 1968. The photograph includes Michael Davies, David Parry, Stephen Lord, Nicholas Jones, Patricia Thomas, Jeffrey Berry, Christine Hickman, Susan Oliver, Brian Thomas. Throughout the years the schools at Maerdy have used Bethania Vestry, Seion Vestry, Ebenezer Vestry (Teify House) and Maerdy Workmen's Hall for lessons, school concerts and festive plays.

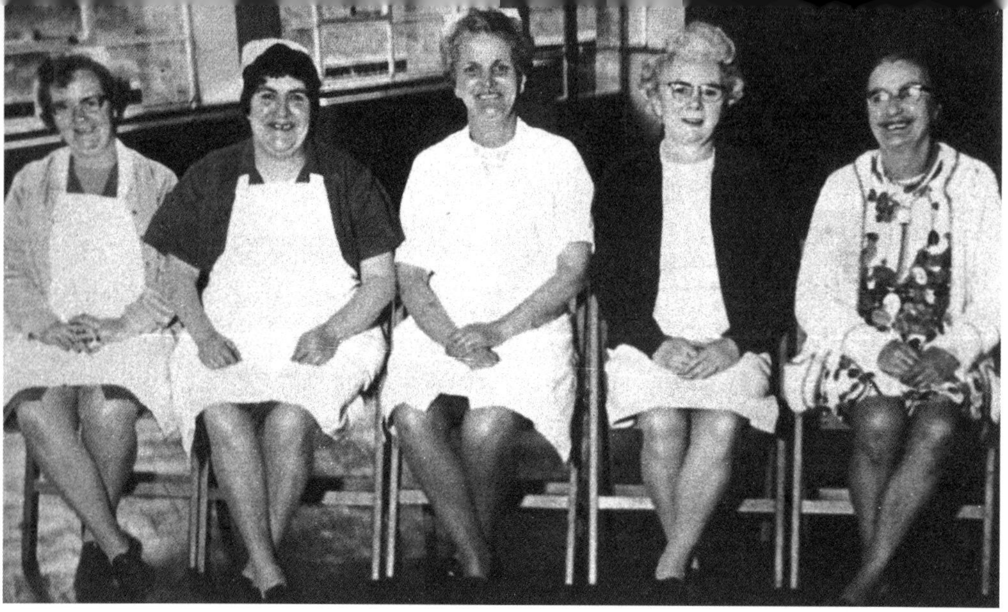

The Junior School Dinner Ladies in 1972. Left to right: Mrs Joan Mellin (asst/cook), Mrs Helen Mellin (asst/cook), Mrs Morwenna Lawes (cook), Mrs Lena Jones (supervisor), Mrs Katy Stevens (supervisor). Pupils have been involved with a Child Safety Internet site and girls in Year 6 attended the World Aerobics Championships in San Francisco.

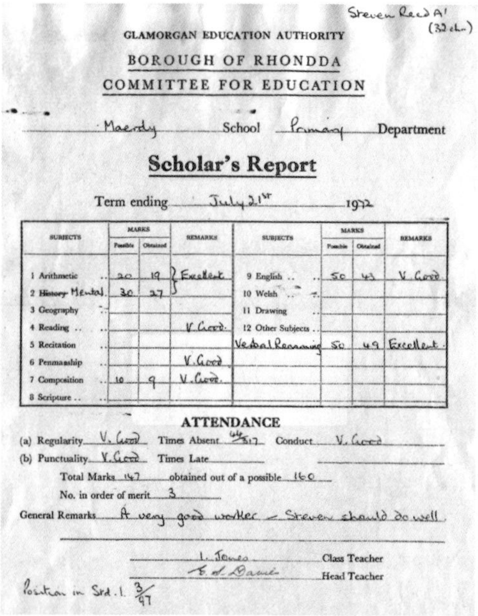

Steven Reed A' (32 ch.)

GLAMORGAN EDUCATION AUTHORITY

BOROUGH OF RHONDDA

COMMITTEE FOR EDUCATION

Maerdy School Primary Department

**Scholar's Report**

Term ending July 21st 1972

| SUBJECTS | MARKS Possible | MARKS Obtained | REMARKS | SUBJECTS | MARKS Possible | MARKS Obtained | REMARKS |
|---|---|---|---|---|---|---|---|
| 1 Arithmetic .. .. | 20 | 19 | } Excellent | 9 English .. .. | 50 | 43 | V. Good |
| 2 ~~History~~ Mental. | 30 | 27 | | 10 Welsh .. .. | | | |
| 3 Geography .. | | | | 11 Drawing .. | | | |
| 4 Reading .. .. | | | V. Good. | 12 Other Subjects .. | | | |
| 5 Recitation .. | | | | Verbal Reasoning | 50 | 49 | Excellent. |
| 6 Penmanship .. | | | V. Good | | | | |
| 7 Composition .. | 10 | 9 | V. Good. | | | | |
| 8 Scripture .. .. | | | | | | | |

**ATTENDANCE**

(a) Regularity V. Good Times Absent 44/317 Conduct V. Good

(b) Punctuality V. Good Times Late

Total Marks 147 obtained out of a possible 160

No. in order of merit 3

General Remarks A very good worker – Steven should do well.

I. Jones Class Teacher

[illegible] Head Teacher

Position in Std. I. 3/47

Left: Steven Reed's Junior School Report 21 July 1972. Right: Carl and Tracy Riddiford Pupils at the Junior School June 1974. Pupils have represented Wales in the Under-11 national football team, represented the LEA in numerous events and held a high profile in the field of Information and Communication Technology.

The Junior School Football Team 1974/75 season. Left to right, back row: Mr John Aeron Lewis (headteacher), Paul Jonathan, David Dean, David Kimber, Gareth Thomas, Jeffery Hill, Hugh Morris (sports teacher). Front row: Vivian Lewis, Andrew Villis, Lee Jenkins, Stewart Voyle, Kevin Bates, Steven Griffiths, Andrew Carlotti.

The Junior School Net Ball Team in 1978. Left to right, back row: Catherine Gallagher, Lynda Thomas, Rhian Cull, Jane King, Carmen Lawes, Tracey Parpworth, -?- Carter, Amanda Evans. Front row: Kathleen Jones, Karen Bates, Nicola Satherly, Angela Maslin, Lynnette Rosser, Beverly Jones, Angela Mullins.

The Junior School Teaching Staff in 1983. Left to right, back row: Mrs Carol Basini, Mr John Morgan, Mr Hugh Morris, Mr Martin Phillips, Mr Peter Blake, Mrs Maureen Williams. Front Row: Mrs Mair Francis, Mrs Irene Jones, Mr John Aeron Lewis (headteacher), Mrs Dorothy Jones, Mrs Veronica Harper.

The Junior School in 1983. Left to right, back row: Mr John Aeron Lewis (headteacher), Geraint Jones, Simon Gravelli, Leigh Jones, Richard Stephens, Dean Gauvain, Dean Wells, Stephen Thomas, Jonathon Cronin, Stephen Harries, Mrs Dorothy Jones (teacher). Middle row: Julie Hayes, Beverly Davies, Georgina Miles, Teresa Marsh, Kathryn Clement, Nicola Wasley, Julie Jones, Cerian Dorrington, Jacqueline Cronin. Front row: Karen Lewis, Shirley Davies, Sara Wharton, Tracey Richardson, Helen Alcock, Michelle Parry, Paula Thomas, Kathryn John, Naomi Stinton, Gwyneth Griffiths.

The Junior School in 1987. Left to right, back row: Jonathan Gill, Craig Davies, Paul Daonie, Lee Jones, Meurig Chapman, Gavin Davies, Mathew Cripps, Ricky Sullivan, Ross Pike, Gareth Beach, Nathan Lewis, Ryan Davies, Marcus Sweet: Middle row: Vicki King, Catherine Leyshon, Heather Pugh, Ceryn Morgan, Hayley Hughes, Mrs Carol Basini (teacher), Kelly Evans, Lisa Blaney, Kelly Jones, Claire Howells, Kerys James. Front row: Clare Kenealy, Sarah Ritchings, Kelly Jones, Kimberly Jones.

The Junior School Dinner Ladies in 1989. Left or right: Mrs Linda Casey (asst/cook), Mrs Carol Jones, Mrs Ruth Griffiths (supervisor), Nell Lawes ('Head Chef' Donny Lawes's dog), Mrs Rosemary Price (cook), Mrs Sheila Holland, Mrs Frances Davies (supervisor), Mrs Patricia Satherly (supervisor), Mrs Helen Goode.

The Junior School Domestic Staff 23 September 1997. Left to right: Mrs B. Evans, Mrs T. Thomas, Mr J. Rowe (caretaker), Mrs D. Evans, Mrs M. Smith. In our school we have fun doing work. In our school we have fun with our friend's wet play or dry. In our school the teacher's are never grumpy. In our school we enjoy doing work from 9:05 till 3:30. Out side our school we have a top yard with lot's of grass. In our school we have a fancy foyer. In our school we have lots of nice people. In our school we have clubs and trip's to enjoy. In our school we have spelling test's every Friday. Charlotte Louise Williams Year 3 Age 8.

The Junior School Class 6w 17 July 1997. Left to right, back row: Mr John Morgan (teacher), Steven Finney, Craig Jones, Michael Evans, Matthew Evans, Theo Morgan, Andrew Pain, Kyle Clements, Steven Jones, Adam Thomas, Mr Peter Blake (headteacher). Middle row: Louise Jonathan, Michela Mackey, Kelly Wells, Louise Earland, Jenna Mason, Lynne Evans, Rachel Rossiter, Amy Blaney, Shaun Bennett. Front row. Michael Jones, Rhys Morris, Kyle Hanson, -?-?- , Aled Woods, Dean Thomas, Carl Pugh, Lee Marsh.

The Junior School Netball Team in 2001. Left to right, back row: Mr Peter Blake (headteacher), Leah Vincent, Claire Moulding, Emma Kinson, Nicki Davies, Natalie Evans, Mrs Julie Kucia (teacher). Front row: Rachel Rowe, Kara Morgan, Daniel Davies, Jessica Richards, Rickelle Earland, Daniel Roberts, Stacey John.

The Junior School 27 March 2002. Assembly is held every morning and is part of the school day when all the children share a precious and momentous time together. Every day a child achieves success at Maerdy Junior School! This year it will celebrate Fifty Years of Maerdy School Days. It is steadfast in the 21st century and is way ahead in multi-media education including interactive white boards used as teaching aids by both staff and pupils as easily as their ancestors used blackboard and chalk. The main hall, corridors and class rooms are splendidly decorated with spacious areas, showing children's photographs, work and paintings; it is a great pleasure just to visit the school.

## Maerdy Junior School Days

*I'll try to tell you a story in poetry or rhyme.
Of school days in Maerdy a very happy time.
The sports days at Maerdy football field.
No other school got their hands on the shield.*

*The winter days when school didn't shut.
The teachers never caught the bus.
Also of sunny days when in yard we play.
Skipping, running and rhyme we would say.*

*There were four hundred and forty pupils in all.
The singing rang from the full school hall.
Hymns and fun songs we did sing.
Very often till playtime bell did ring.*

*How many teachers do you remember?
Several I think from four Septembers.
There were Mr and Mrs Evans, John and Harper
Several Joneses too did one of them teach you.*

*The concert in the chapel children singing loud,
The parents filled the seats further down.
We sang with gusto and with glee,
We knew we would have a late morning you see.*

*Mrs Aileen John conducted us like a choir,
She made the boys sing higher and higher.
The little white bull did ring out,
The teachers also knew how loud to shout.*

*I look back and think of times pass
Sitting in the bottom wing class.
Trips to the zoo and caves we made,
For these trips you could save.*

*The junior school at eleven years we left,
Not having any more to climb the steps.
Now I can look back years after,
Thinking of many years of laughter.*

*Edith Kempton Age 44 of Griffiths Street*

## Junior School!!

*On a hill far away,
Stands a school all alone,
With smiles and memories
Of four years almost gone.*

*I arrived at Maerdy Juniors
Amongst great excitement and wonder,
New teachers to meet
Mr Blake we'd rule under.*

*To assembly each morning
We walk in single file
To sing with vigour and strength
Smiles beaming all the while.*

*Corridor walls covered in photos
Of faces old and new
Of sports days and such occasions
I can assure you there's been a few.*

*Christmas is a special time
And for our plays we are well known
Mr Rowe is the man to trim the tree
He does the job alone.*

*My teacher I think she's the best
Mrs Kucia is her name
She's funny, kind and generous
And treats us all the same.*

*I hate to leave this lovely place
And yet I must move on
Thank you for making me who I am
Sensible, kind and strong.*

*Sophie Jane Hopkins Year 6 Age 11*

## *Four*

# The Community School

A large imposing building has been defiantly sitting on a flat piece of land in Maerdy for about 32 years. Nestling between two steep parallel mountain slopes at the 'lower end' of Maerdy deep in the Rhondda Fach. The school has undergone many transformations during this time, both physically, culturally and sociologically, to become the local Community School in its present form.

On 3 November 1969, it started life as a Grammar School, continuing until September 1973 when it evolved into a brand new Comprehensive, soon to become referred to as 'Maerdy Comp' or simply 'the comp'. This establishment was presided over by the first headmaster Mr Kenneth Hopkins who held power from 1969-1971 was followed by Mr John Kenneth Harper 1971-1983.

Then it was the turn of Mr Andrew John George Chinn to take the reins during some of the greatest upheavals the school has ever witnessed, caused mainly by two devastating fires.

Uncannily, the first fire occurred exactly 21 years to the day that the school site first opened, that day being 3 November 1990. The second fire took hold a year later during Whitsuntide 1991. As a result, a huge section of the building was razed to the ground with several departments totally obliterated. Staff, parents and pupils were shocked and devastated, with huge amounts of examination work destroyed in one night. However, the spirit of the school proved too strong to be diminished, and it was not too long before lessons reached some kind of normality with pupils being taught in alternative rooms, and even the dining hall was utilized for several weeks by the art department. The phrase 'community spirit' was never more poignant at that time! Cutting a very long story short, it must be said that one of the great 'advantages' of the fire was the development of a new multi-million pound complex, which assured the survival of the school for years to come. Also, there would no longer be a necessity for pupils to be farmed-out to other schools throughout the Valleys, and they could still be educated virtually on their own doorsteps.

Mr Chinn left in 1996 to be replaced by Mr Robert Meier, who in turn, is succeeded by the new head Mr Peter Jenkins.

Lately, links with the wider community are being made even stronger, bolstered by a succession of award evenings, fetes, open days, parent evenings and many other events. The publication of a new termly Community newsletter is now, informing the entire catchment area of all the positive achievements of the pupils. So we continue to progress into the future!

When I started teaching at this school in 1975, I was advised by colleagues to move-on every five years to maintain a fresh approach to the job. I am glad that like many other staff, I stayed, because all the changes, challenges and innumerable situations that any teacher needs to remain 'fresh' have taken place under one roof and in one establishment, namely the local Community School, constantly evolving to the benefit of all concerned.

Mr Thomas Alan Morgan Art Teacher at the Community School

The Construction Gang in 1969. Left to right, back row: Dai Jones, Cyril Evans, Larry Satherly, Billy Lewis, Viv Paul, John Miles. Front row: Mike Davies, Brian Evans, Idris James (carpenter), Meirion 'Milky Bar' Thomas, Mr Jones, Eddie Dibbs, Neville Morris. Since the school began the staff, children, governors, parents and local people of the community have raised thousands of pounds to benefit the school and the children in their education. Thanks must be given to one and all that have given their time and help in any way, little or large, over the past thirty three years. There is a small account in the following chapter of some achievements and money raised for the school.

## The Community School Headteachers from 1969 to date

| | | |
|---|---|---|
| 1969 | 1971 | Mr Kenneth Hopkins |
| 1971 | 1983 | Mr John Kenneth Harper |
| 1983 | 1996 | Mr Andrew John George Chinn |
| 1996 | 2001 | Mr Robert Meier |
| 2001 | (to date) | Mr Peter Jenkins |

The focus for our work is of course the pupils at the Community School and we intend to recognise and record their experiences and successes. We firmly believe that everyone should be aware of the schools achievements and would wish to join with us in celebration. Far too often these days it is the negative aspects of our youth that are highlighted. Therefore, the staff aims to provide a far more accurate picture that shows we have every reason to be proud of our young people. Mr Peter Jenkins (headteacher).

Pupil Ryan Bartlett wrote a poem for the Millennium. After reading Ryan's poem, Cardiff Lord Mayor Councillor Russell Goodway invited him to spend a day experiencing life in the corridors of power. 'My dream is to become the Mayor of Cardiff'. I would ask the Government for money to make Cardiff one of the great cites of the world. I would start with a council to run South Wales and make the standard of living very good and crime would be very low. Education and healthcare would be the best in Britain. And I would have sports academies to make Wales a great sporting nation. I would then be able to retire to a house in Cardiff Bay with a job well done.

The Community School. In 1971 each school form was named with the letters that spelled Bryngoleu Crescent where headteacher Mr John Kenneth Harper lived.

## *Maerdy School Days*

*School, School, School*
*Where do I start?*
*With old rotten porta-cabins*
*And basketball rings in the barn*
*Smart clever art rooms*
*A small neat dining room*
*Ready for the dinnertime rush*
*A million different bossy teachers*
*Who don't give you a rest*
*But I can cope……*
*I Suppose!*

*Grace Leyshon Year 7IS Age 12*

## *Dyddiau Ysgol Maerdy*

*Ysgol, Ysgol, Ysgol*
*Ble alla i ddechrau?*
*Gyda hen gabanau symudol pwdr*
*Cylchoedd pêl fasged yn yr ysgubor*
*Ystafelloedd celf twt a dawnus*
*Ystafell fwyta fach a thaclus*
*Yn barod am lif amser cinio*
*Miloedd o athrawon gwahanol*
*Sy'n cadw chi'n brysur*
*Ond gallaf ymdopi……*
*Sïwr o fod!*

*Grace Leyshon Blwyddyn 7IS Oedran 12*

My mind goes back to the years 1972-1973 when a considerable number of additional teachers were appointed as members of Staff for the new Comprehensive School which was to be opened in September, 1973. That year, I was Chairman of the Governing Body which was involved in these preparations. I remember that we, as a body, interviewed more than thirty teachers for various teaching posts for the new Comprehensive School.

In September, 1973, Ferndale North Road Boys' School (already housed in the former Ferndale Grammar School), Ferndale Dyffryn Girls' School, Tylorstown Hendrefadog Mixed School and existing Grammar School pupils joined together to form the new Comprehensive School. The lower forms were accommodated in the former Grammar School building and the Dyffryn School, while the middle and upper forms were in the new Comprehensive School. The aim of the comprehensive system was to ensure that there were better facilities with a large, proficient, well qualified Staff in a school catering not only for the more academic pupils but also helping to develop the talents and interests of the less academic students and encouraging all pupils in the fields best suited to their abilities. Hon Alderman Glyn James.

Left: The Community School 'Head of All Caretakers' Dilwyn Llewellyn. Dilwyn was caretaker from 1969 to 2001. Right: Mr John Hatch is now the new 'Head of All Caretakers' and has worked at the school for more years than he cares to remember. He now has the pleasure of living 'on site' at the community school caretaker's house.

The Community School in 1977. The photograph includes: Maureen Gwynn, Michael Gregory, Paul Daniels, Malcolm Gregory, Adrian Chard, Gareth Thomas, Christopher Burgoyne, Maureen Brown, Julie Sweet, Susan Thomas, Jacqueline Downs, Kay Sweet, Mrs Carol Jones (teacher). Pupils have the opportunity to participate in mock interviews. First they complete an application form; they are then given a letter stating where the interview was to take place, the time to arrive and with whom. They are then interviewed by personnel from various walks of life including the Inland Revenue, the Fire Service and the Armed Forces etc.

The Community School Form 4e in 1981. The photograph includes: Richard Rees, Alison Griffiths, Tracey Mathews, Donna Dean, Paula Lewis, Irene Tudor, Michelle Evans. Over a hundred students received their 'Records of Achievement' which catalogue their successes throughout their school lives, not only academically, but also in activities such as the Duke of Edinburgh Award Scheme and team sports.

The Community School Fete in 1981. Left to right: Russell, John and Stewart Barnes. The school building in the background of the photograph was destroyed by fire on 3 November 1990. Students are able to find out about the courses on offer at Cardiff University. They have the opportunity to talk with first year students regarding the social life and the inspiration to work hard to achieve the necessary grades!

The Community School Headteacher Mr Andrew John George Chinn (1983/1996) is planting a tree in the school grounds. Maerdy Youth Club has embarked on an ambitious garden project, which will involve the pupils of the Community School. Plans have been drawn up by the Groundwork Trust to transform the spare land between the youth club and lower school buildings. The area is to be landscaped and entered into an environmental project competition.

The Community School Headteacher Mr Robert Meier (1996/2001) is presiding over assembly. The Community School's new headteacher Mr Peter Jenkins has a high regard for his pupils. He replaced Robert Meier at the start of the autumn term in 2001 and was eager to sing the school's praises. "I accepted the job because it had a reputation for caring for its pupils and the culture of expecting them to achieve", he said. "It has already had excellent results thanks to the commitment of its staff. Now it is simply up to me to ensure it stays that way, and if possible improve further".

The Community School Form 3 in 1982. Left to right, back row: G. 'Reesy' Thomas, S. Jones, R. Jones, C. 'Gren' Green, M. Bailey, M. 'Mickey' Jones, G. 'Gaffa Trev' Thomas, A. 'Aggis' Harris, -?-?-. Middle row: -?-?-, K. Gravell, L. McKendley, M. Varney, D. Moulding, C. Abbot, R. 'Hicksy' Hicks, M. 'Chimsy' Clement, M. 'Britt' Britten. Front row: R. Vaja, L. Holland, K. McPhail, C. Evans, Mr. Thomas Alan Morgan (teacher), B. Jones, D. Adams, N. Jeffreys, L. Edgell.

The Community School in 1984. The photograph includes: Michael Bidiscombe, Jason Evans, Carl Prawl, Debbie French, Jason Pike, Debbie Evans, Katherine Clements, Maria Richards, Natalie Beazley, Suzanne Collins, Caroline Hughes, Mr John Elwyn Jones (teacher). Rebecca Podmore, a Year 7 Pupil, took part in a competition organised by Maerdy Library, to encourage young people to read. As the most prolific reader, Rebecca was awarded a medal by the Library Services.

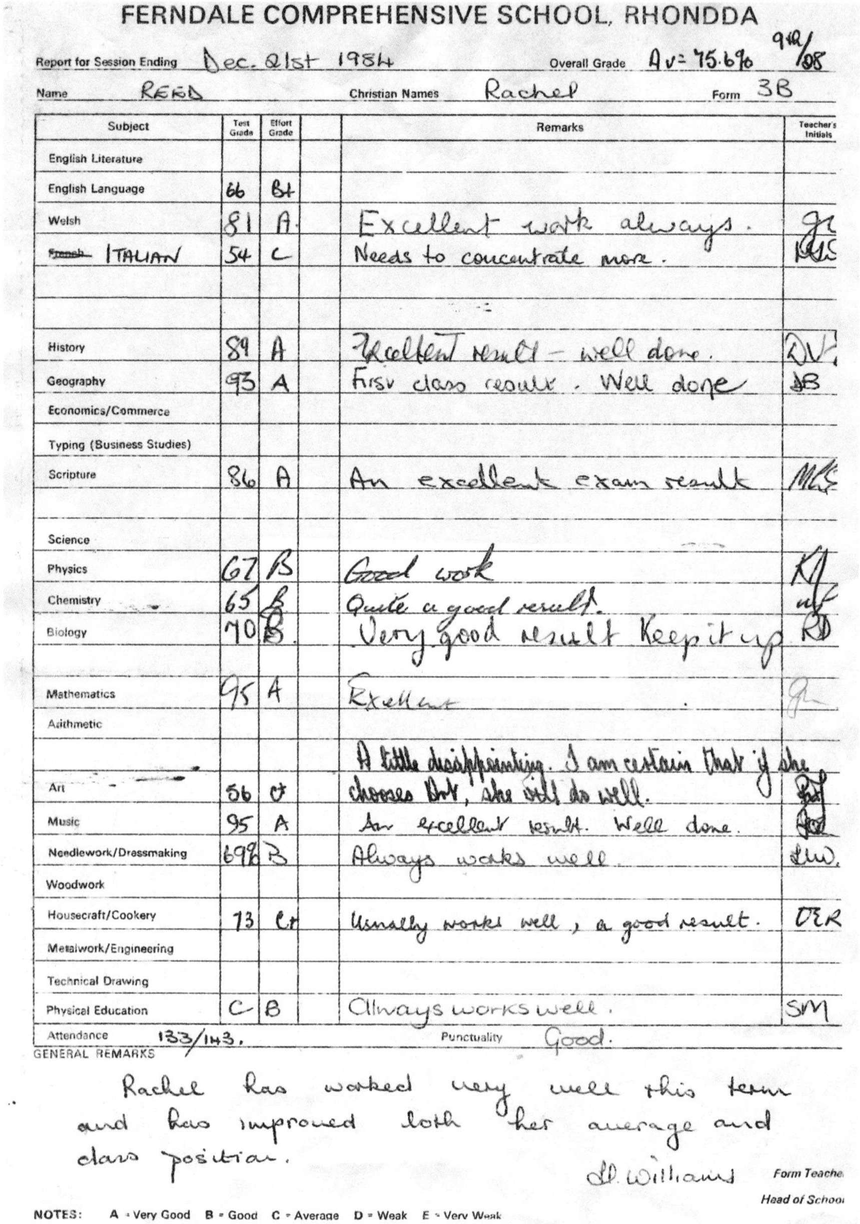
FERNDALE COMPREHENSIVE SCHOOL, RHONDDA

Report for Session Ending Dec. 21st 1984 Overall Grade Av= 75.6% 9th/28

Name REED Christian Names Rachel Form 3B

| Subject | Test Grade | Effort Grade | Remarks | Teacher's Initials |
|---|---|---|---|---|
| English Literature | | | | |
| English Language | 66 | B+ | | |
| Welsh | 81 | A | Excellent work always. | [illegible] |
| ~~French~~ ITALIAN | 54 | C | Needs to concentrate more. | [illegible] |
| | | | | |
| | | | | |
| History | 89 | A | Excellent result – well done. | [illegible] |
| Geography | 93 | A | First class result. Well done | [illegible] |
| Economics/Commerce | | | | |
| Typing (Business Studies) | | | | |
| Scripture | 86 | A | An excellent exam result | [illegible] |
| | | | | |
| Science | | | | |
| Physics | 67 | B | Good work | [illegible] |
| Chemistry | 65 | B | Quite a good result. | [illegible] |
| Biology | 70 | B | Very good result Keep it up | [illegible] |
| | | | | |
| Mathematics | 95 | A | Excellent | [illegible] |
| Arithmetic | | | | |
| | | | A little disappointing. I am certain that if she | |
| Art | 56 | C+ | chooses Art, she will do well. | [illegible] |
| Music | 95 | A | An excellent result. Well done. | [illegible] |
| Needlework/Dressmaking | 69% | B | Always works well | LW. |
| Woodwork | | | | |
| Housecraft/Cookery | 73 | C+ | Usually works well, a good result. | [illegible] |
| Metalwork/Engineering | | | | |
| Technical Drawing | | | | |
| Physical Education | C | B | Always works well. | SM |

Attendance 133/143. Punctuality Good.

GENERAL REMARKS

Rachel has worked very well this term and has improved both her average and class position.

Ll. Williams Form Teacher

Head of School

NOTES: A = Very Good B = Good C = Average D = Weak E = Very Weak

Rachel Reed formerly of Richard Street, Maerdy, School Report, Form 3b, Term ending 21 December 1984. The first edition of the school newsletter was a roaring success, with parents and the local community offering very positive feedback. People were delighted to hear of the pupils' many and varied achievements. The magazine mirrors just a fraction of the good things that go on in the school. Mr Peter Blake, Headteacher of Maerdy Junior School wrote a letter expressing his delight in being able to keep track of some of his former pupils' progress, and he looked forward to the next publication. My thanks to all those who have willingly contributed to this new and revealing venture. Mr Thomas Alan Morgan (teacher).

The Community School Dinner Ladies in 1989. The school meals staff working in the upper department of the school raised £1,277-24p for the Lord Tonypandy Macmillan Fund. The photograph includes: Mrs Evelyn Williams, Mrs Georgina Harries, Mr John Aeron Lewis, Mrs Phyllis Thomas, Mrs Iris Pitman, Mrs Margaret Thomas, Mrs Margaret Casey, Mrs Jennifer Morgan, Mrs Eunice Rees, Mrs Thelma Hughes, Mrs Jean Hopkins, Mrs Dorothy Davies.

The Community School Dinner Ladies in 1989. The school meals staff working in the lower department of the school. The photograph includes: Mrs Pat Williams, Mrs Thelma Hughes, Mrs Gina Harris, Mrs Lillian Thomas, Mrs Jean Hopkins, Mrs Sonia Carter, Mrs Dorothy Davies. The school dinner ladies enjoy serving up a feast for the pupils. Their meals are a credit to the school.

The Community School on fire 3 November 1990. A huge section of the building was razed to the ground with several departments totally obliterated, with huge amounts of examination work destroyed in one night. However, the spirit of the school proved too strong to be diminished, and it was not too long before lessons reached some kind of normality with pupils being taught in alternative rooms even the dining hall. The phrase 'community spirit' was never more poignant at that time!

The Community School being rebuilt in 1991. One of the great advantages of the fire was the development of a new multi-million pound complex, which assured the survival of the school for years to come. Also, there would no longer be a necessity for pupils to be farmed-out to other schools throughout the Valleys, and they could still be educated virtually on their own doorsteps.

The Community School Staff in 1996. The photograph includes: Mr E. James, Mr S. Brooks, Mr M. Price, Mr J. Rowe, Mr K. Wigley, Mr I. Evans, Mrs L. Stoyle, Mrs A. Harries, Mrs D. Thomas, Miss P. Morgan, Mr S. Keeble, Mr D. Jenkins, Mr T.A. Morgan, Mr G. Jones, Mr P. Griffin, Mr R. W. Jones, Mr W. Price, Mrs C. Reed, Mrs C. Jones, Mrs J. Treeby, Mrs C. Evans, Mrs J. Price, Mr J. Hatch, Mrs M. Harries, Mr K. Jenkins, Mr R. Whitmore, Mr W.L. Jones, Mrs G. McGrath, Mrs C. Jones, Mr P. Kiff, Mr B. Jones, Mr R. Emblin, Mrs V. Condon, Mr D. Llewellyn, Mrs G. Morgan, Mrs J. Higgins, Mrs N. Meredith, Mrs N. Chaffe, Mrs K. Williams, Mrs S. Allen, Mrs S. Jones, Mrs A. Pilliner, Mr B. Davies, Mr R. Gough, Mrs L. Robbins, Mrs K. Jones, Mrs K. Evans, Mrs D. Jones, Mrs M. Evans, Mrs J. Patrick, Mrs J. L'Homme, Mrs V. Leyshon, Mrs G. Knight, Mrs S. Parry, Mrs M. Burridge, Mrs A. Hemmings, Mrs J. Pearce, Mrs M. Gwyn, Mrs C. Richards, Mrs M. Shotton, Miss C. Stephens, Mrs E. Palmer, Mrs H. Williams, Mrs A. Grover, Mrs J. Inglis, Miss S. Evans, Mrs T. Jones, Mrs M. Griffiths, Mrs V. Wiltshire, Mrs R. Davies, Mr M.L. Evans, Mr R. Inder, Mr C. Clements, Mr D.C. Jones, Mrs J. Ryan, Mr D.V. Evans, Mr. Andrew John George Chinn (headteacher), Mr J.A. Edmunds, Mrs H. Paul, Mr R. Hughes, Mr L.H. Gibbins, Mr G. Richards, Mr K. Ellis, Mrs T. Truscott.

**F**CS is a funny old school, **E**very day pupils learn
**R**ead and write, **N**ever do they mess around
**D**oing their homework every night, **A**ll the pupils enjoy biology
**L**eaving school isn't a misery. **E**lectric plugs in physics.
**C**hemicals in chemistry. **O**n Tuesdays everyone likes drama.
**M**ondays everyone hates, **M**aybe everyone likes art.
**U**nless it's cancelled. **N**ever has PE gone down,
**I**t helps us get fit. **T**eachers go home with a big hip hooray
**Y**et, they have the rest of the week to conquer. **S**cary dreams the,
**C**hildren have until the school **H**olidays come, then they'll be dancing in the rain
**O**nly the day they're dreading. **O**ne day until the school holidays are over
**L**ate in the night they finish they're homework.

Sarah Harris Year 7GI Age 12

Community School Pupils Glen Jenkins and Angela Treeby in the Science Department in 1997. A-level wizards; Angela Treeby and Leanne Maddox achieved the best A level results. Sports star Bethan Sweet and Matthew Harrison won the Lisa Gibbins Memorial Award. Guest speakers were RCT Group Director of Education and children services Dewi Jones, and former pupil Nicola Jones, now the Finance Manager for the Cardiff and Vale Trust. They presented COFA, GGSE, GCE and GNVQ certificates for Young Enterprise and Dragon Sports.

The Community School Eisteddfod in 1997. The photograph includes: Laura Gaspar, Lyndsay Carter, Claire Treeby, Laura Davies, Katrina Pavlovic, Aimee Jeffries, Nadia Emblin. You never know what you're going to experience whenever you enter the Drama Department. Mr Simon Keeble (drama teacher) has managed to tap a rich vein of acting talent throughout the entire age range of the school, and even manages to get staff involved on certain occasions. His major productions are well known in the community.

The Community School Shakespearean Play, Merchant of Venice in the 1970s. The photograph includes: R. Thomas, J. Addison, K. Adams, S. Williams, M. Thomas, M. Hall, R. Tann, S. Seal, G. Holloway, C. Hobbs, E. Addison, C. Lewis, A. Walker, D. Smart, J. Humphreys, G. Ellis, N. Rees, Mr John Evans (teacher), Mr John Kenneth Harper (headteacher), G. Rees, J. Williams, J. Condon. In 2001 Karl Jenkins and Craig Morris were head and deputy head boy, while Ria James and Judie Edwards were head and deputy head girl. Mr Peter Jenkins (headteacher) said: "The pupils' performance has been exceptional. It reflects the hard work done by the majority of the students".

Left: Mr Simon Keeble (drama teacher). Rhys' Secret, an historical bloodthirsty romp set in Norman times, which was based on the true story of the Conquest of Glamorgan by Sir John Fitzhanon in 1093, and his battle with the Welsh Kings (namely some of the staff!). Right: Tyrone Jones, Richard Williams. The play included some thrilling bloodthirsty moments, there were gasps from the audience when Rhys laid down to be beheaded, and a dummy head was raised for all to see. Everyone awaits the next block buster!

The Community School Sports Day at the Darran Park in 1997. The photograph includes: Mr Gerwyn Clement (teacher), Mr Thomas Alan Morgan (teacher), Mr Wynford Price (teacher), Mr Paul Griffin (teacher). Rhondda schools have had the best ever presentation at international level over the last couple of years. Craig Morris (Community School) had an impressive game at number 8 for Wales Under-16s against England at Rodney Parade Newport. He made several telling breaks and set up a try for Wales' victory. Well done boys and all involved, Rhondda schools are proud of your well deserved achievements.

The Community School Cross Country League Champions 1986/1987, 1987/1988. Left to right, back row: Darren Thomas, Adrian and Andrew Crabb. Front row: Lance Worthington, Paul Morris, Karl Middleton. Girls from the Community School enjoyed a day with members of the Rhondda Rebels basket ball team as part of the wise for Life project. The project, enable the pupils to receive expert basketball coaching and face the problem-solving exercises away from the basket ball court.

Left: Rebecca Chick hurling the discus at the Community School Sports Day in 1997. Right: Kelly Davies in the relay at the Community School Sports Day in 1997. Pupils had a devil of a time when two ice hockey players paid them a visit. Cardiff Devils stars Merv Preest and Phil Hill took some time to chat to pupils. Year 7 Pupil Liam Jones tried on a Cardiff Devil kit.

Mathew Thomas in the high jump at the Community School Sports Day in 1997. Pupil Rhian Jones is aiming for Athens 2004. Rhian was born with a congenital deformity and had part of her right leg amputated at the age of six, doctor suggested to join the local swimming club to strengthen her legs. What began as a physiotherapy soon became a passion. At the age of 12 she was asked to join the BYT Welsh Disable Swimming Squad and in her first national heat, scooped five gold medals.

The Community School Sports Day in 1997. The photograph includes: Pupils Dean Clemence, James Thomas, Lee Burridge taking a breather in the pool. Rhian now trains with Rhondda Swimming Club and competes in both national and international competition for Wales and hopes to compete in the Commonwealth Games next year. She will soon be heading off to university to study English and hope to become a primary school teacher in the future.

Left: Mark Woodmass in the Relay at the Community School Sports Day in 1997. Right: Hannah Szigetvari Welsh Cap for Women's Rugby in 2001. Hannah has been selected for the Under-16 Woman's Welsh rugby squad. Earlier this year she represented East Wales in a regional match against West Wales and has now been selected for the first ever Wales Under-16 squad.

Left: Mathew Holland in 2002. Mathew has played for Maerdy Under-11, and now plays for the Under-15, Rhondda and Pontypridd schools. He is now on a six week trial with Swansea City Football Club. Right: Luke Davies in 2002. Luke Welsh Bowls Under-16 Singles and Triples Champion. Luke is a member of the Maerdy Park Bowls Club.

Left: Adam Thomas in 2002. Adam has been selected for the Welsh schools Rugby Union Under-16 squad. He is a good all round athlete and has also represented the County in swimming. He will undertake a tour to Italy with the Welsh squad this year. Right: Rupert Moon Welsh rugby international pops in to chat to Compact Award Winners in 2002. The photograph includes: Stacey Jenkins, Samantha Griffiths.

Left: Class of 97 Oxbridge Successes in 1997. Left to right: Lynette Mason, Ryan Evans, Joanne Clement. Right: Young Consumers in 2002. Left to right: Nadia Thirb, Laura Lewis, Louise Blaney (captain), Hayley Davies. The pupils swept to victory and the school received a prize of £200 and each team member £20 in vouchers and individual trophies.

Left: Kalum Jones Rhondda Rotary Club Young Chef in 2001. Kalum had to cook a two-course meal for two people for under £7-50p. With remarkable resourcefulness Kalum prepared a Creamed Fisherman's Pie followed by Pears in a Blackcurrant Coulis. Right: Lindsay Edwards Rhondda Rotary Young Chef in 2002. Lindsay cooked a meal of Japanese rolled pork in plum sauce for a starter, frittata for the main course and lemon syllabub for dessert. Lindsay is through to the Welsh finals, to be held later in 2002.

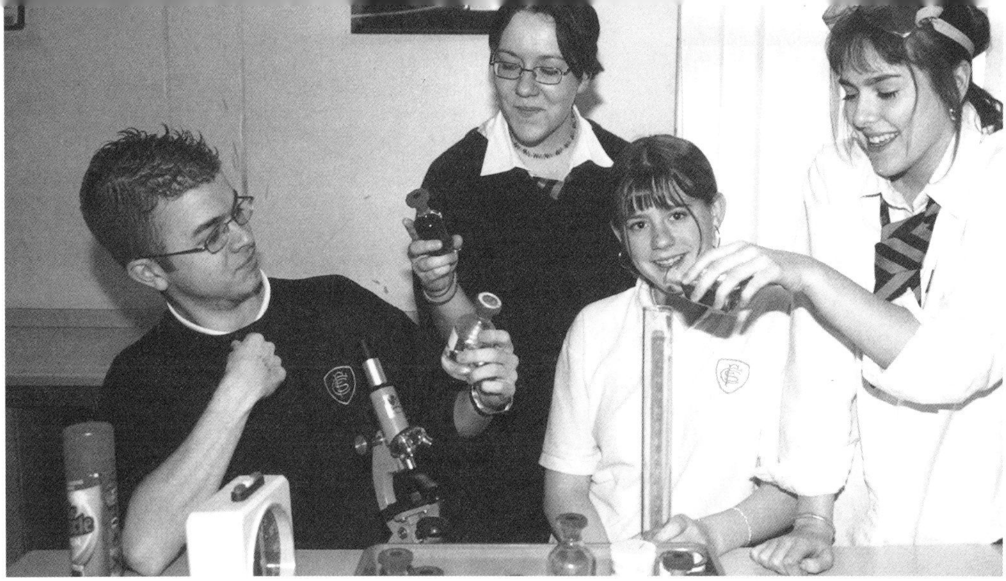

The Community School in 2002. Left to right: Michael John (occupational therapy), Rebecca Smith (occupational therapy), Jennifer Thomas (occupational therapy), Emily England (physiotherapy). Five Year 11 Pupils have been successful in gaining a place on the University of Wales, College of Medicine, Compact Scheme. This will give the pupils an opportunity to learn more about Health Care courses at the University.

The Community School in 2002. Left to right, back row: J. Howells, S. King, M. John. Front row: B. Rees, K. Combellack, Mrs Lynne Robbins (teacher), A. Morgan, G. Hopkins. Over 30% of the pupils in Year 11 have already achieved a grade C or better in GCSE Maths. Approximately 40% of the year group sat the GCSE Maths last June or November. The high pass rate was entirely due to the willingness of the pupils to attend after school lessons and the extra voluntary work put in by their teachers, Mr Richard Gough and Mrs Lynne Robbins.

The Community School in 2001. Students celebrate successes at the School Ball. Left to right: Gemma Williams, Hannah L'Homme, Laura Clement. This year sees the 80th birthday of HRH the Duke of Edinburgh. The Awards scheme is celebrating 45 years of challenging and developing youngsters' skills and confidence. Five youngsters from RCT will be representing the borough at the Duke of Edinburgh's birthday party held at the Royal Albert Hall at London.

The Community School Year 6 in 2001. The photograph includes: J. John, M. John, M. Harrison, C. Williams, O. Rees, W. Herbert, J. Comey, C. Baker, M. Owens, L. Palmer, B. Franks, K. Mon, D. Parfitt, M. Evans, R. Edwards, L. Gwyn, M. Hadfield, C. Jenkins, M. Fry, G. Smith, R. Jones, L. Davies, C. John, V. Gabriel, L. Carter, J. Lewis, L. Davies, R. Traylor, M. Fry, R. Williams, D. Holmes, L. Davies, C. Harries, G. Allen, S. Price, K. Facey.

The Community School in 2001. Left to right: Nadia Thirb, Hayley Davies, Rochelle Bryant and Bethan Evans with students from Cardiff University. A large vehicle arrived at the school but within minutes it was transformed into an exciting information centre. The representatives of Cardiff University then invited Years 11 and 12 to find out about university life, including, courses, funding and living arrangements.

Left: The Community School in 2002. Left to right: Carrie Jones, Kieran Richards Year 7. Religious Education will never be the same for Carrie Jones and Kieran Richards, who took a prominent part in an active learning lesson on Hinduism. As part of a multi-cultural awareness programme, teacher Mrs Lisa Codd introduced the pupils to many aspects of this colourful religion through a series of dramatic and written exercises. Pupils dressed in traditional costume and re-enacted some Hindu ceremonies. Class assembly is held every morning for year groups and school assembly is held every month where all the pupils in the school are packed tightly together in the upper school hall. Visiting guests include vicars and priests of all dominations.

The Community School in 1998. Left to right: A. Jenkins, C. Dawns, M. Jenkins, M. Pugh, G. Ellis. Pupils A. Butler, P. Darch, R. Williams and S. Morgans raised £500 for the LEPRA charity by showing off their Karaoke skills. LEPRA works to help and cure people who suffer from leprosy all over the world. Just £21 can provide a complete cure for one person.

The Community School in 2001. National Poetry Day provided a day of learning and fundraising. Left to right, back row: Taryl Thomas, Stephen Jones, Mrs Janet Inglis (teacher), Rickelle Earland, Jessica Clarke. Front row: Calvin Williams, Nicola Ward, Tina McKendley. Friends and families sponsored their efforts.

Left: Mark Jones dishing out pop and crisps at the school Fete in 2000. The fete was a great success for organiser veteran teacher (45 years) Mrs Mary Shotton. The Fete raised around £2,000. Right: Emma Jones, Gethin Jones, Dylan Thompson raising loads of money for Children in Need in 2000. Every year, the fun, filled madness of children in need is thrust upon the school. It is a chance for people young and old to let down their hair (if they have any left) for charity. For many years the school have raised thousands of pounds for Children in Need.

The Community School in 2001. Just before Christmas, Head girl Ria James was so moved by the plight of children in dire need around the world that she became heavily involved in 'Operation Christmas Child' - an organisation that helps light up the lives of young children who have suffered through war, poverty, natural disasters or neglect. Her hard work and persistence resulted in almost 200 packages being sent to the charity.

The Community School National Poetry Day in 2001. Left to right: Calvin Williams, Nicola Ward, Tina McKendley. There are some days when you get up, draw back the curtains and instinctively know that the next few hours are going to be very satisfying. During the days prior to the poetry day, pupils prepared poems on theme of 'Journeys' in Welsh, English and French. Friends and families sponsored their efforts and raised £570.

The Community School in 2001. The photograph includes: S. Parlour, G. Bradfield, M. Burroughs, D. Evans, D. Rees, K. Isaac. The 'Team' pupils got a taste of life in the 'in industry' morning. Year 10 and 11 Pupils learned the importance of key skills and how they apply to future jobs from local companies and organisations. Representatives of HSBC, Barclays Bank, GE Aircraft, South Wales Police, Fire Service and the Army spent the morning with the pupils, bringing them up to date and answering questions.

The Community School sponsored walk in 2001. The photograph includes: Mr Phillip Kiff (technology teacher), Daniel Coleman, Carl Hallet, Cara Moulding, Kelly Isaac, Jenna Ford, Joanne Cox, Amy Bolderson, Jade Lewis, Michael Burrough, Joseph Margery, Katy Bromage, Kayleigh Morgans, Danielle Rees, Sarah Jacobs. More than 250 joined together to walk the streets from Maerdy to Tylorstown, and for their pains raised a staggering £1,000. This annual event is always a great success and great fun!

The Community School in 2002. Rhondda Special School's Bank balance has increased by £230 thanks to Community School student Leah Llewellyn. Leah front left in the photograph organised a non-uniform day and class-by-class collections to raise the money. She presented the cheque to Rhondda Special School headteacher Mr Andy Henderson during a special assembly at his school. The school was very proud of her efforts.

The Community School in 2002. Left to right: Kaylie Hamm, Elizabeth Pavlovic. The school celebrated the fifth successful year of its paired reading programme. The scheme teams up Year 7 children with older reading 'Butties' from Year 12. The system gives younger children help and support in their transition from primary to secondary school, allowing them to make friends as well as improve their reading. The older pupils also benefit from the experience of working with others, especially those who wish to pursue a career in teaching or childcare.

The Community School in 2002. Left to right: Mrs Marilyn Evans (special needs support teacher), Simon Bould. Children from Trealaw Special School have been attending the school for a variety of mainstream experiences. They are enjoying themselves in a wide-range of learning activities with other children, including, art, computer studies, PE and several literary projects. The children are being accompanied by Mrs Marilyn Evans (teacher) and Mrs Salisbury (teacher), who both agree that, to date, the initiative has proven very successful with teachers and pupils gaining a great deal from the experience.

The Community School achievements have been celebrated with jubilation and delight in the past 33 years. The future is secure and cheerfully bright under the guidance of the school staff. Dance was on the agenda when the union dance company put pupils through their paces. Students then had the chance to see the dance company perform the same steps they had learned, at a performance at the Taliesin Theatre, Swansea. Pupils study dance as part of the curriculum.

The Community School relives the past with Mr David Clwyd Jones (teacher). Remember the Cane? I certainly do. Some Whipper Ins (welfare officers) were also known to carry the dreaded cane. They say schooldays are the happiest of your life but this class would not agree. Mr William David 'Will Dai' Evans (teacher) formerly at the Elementary Boys School taught English and Maths 'with severe efficiency'. The cane has now become a punishment and memory of bygone days.

An Aerial View of the Community School. The school is situated in the centre of the photograph. Visitors to the school will have seen considerable changes in recent months and I am delighted to say that these will continue in the coming year. A significant sum of money is to be spent on refurbishing a number of our buildings. The extra monies provided by RCT that will enable us to do this is greatly appreciated and will help ensure that the children of this valley have the quality of environment to which they are entitled. A quality education is an entitlement to every child. He is also keen to establish a community school where adults can return to education alongside the pupils. "If anyone wants to come in and join a class during the day, then please come and let me know" he said. "We already have one student who has taken up A level Geography and sits with a sixth-former". Most importantly, he is keen to encourage stronger relationships between the schools, its pupils and their parents. "Believe in the partnership between parents and the school", he said. "Our jobs are made far easier with their support. Mr Peter Jenkins Headteacher 2002.

**Future Rhondda Cynon Taff Schools Days**

Rhondda Cynon Taff March 2002. Construction on new replacement schools has started and £25 million more is going to be invested in better school buildings soon. A significant sum of money is to be spent on refurbishing a number of buildings at the Community School. Contractors moved on site at Baglan Fields in Treherbert to build a new Community Primary School at a cost of £1.8 million. Work also started recently on a new £2.3 million Welsh Medium Primary School for 290 children at Aberdare. Next – a new Special School at Ystrad. Plans include 12 classrooms, a parents' room and a hydrotherapy pool. The building programme will maintain this level of investment in the children's future.

Up 7% double the average increase in Wales. Pupils with 5 or more GCSE passes at Grades A*-C up 22%. Double Wales average increase in pupils with 5 or more GCSE grades A*-C above Wales average scores – English, Maths, science. Welsh for 11-year-olds. A* is the ultimate grade.

We congratulate the entire staff and pupils at Maerdy for their work and dedication and we extend heartiest congratulations to the pupils on their remarkable successes in examinations and sport a truly great achievement. We wish them all success for the future, in pursuing their goal and to follow the generations of children who have been educated in the schools at Maerdy with many going on to Universities, distinguished careers and professions.

## Maerdy School Days

Teachers shout like roaring bears,
"Get up! Turn around! Be quiet"!
Like fierce tigers prowling a dark forest.
First they look at your hard work.
Then they go and have a sit down.
They keep their eyes on all the class.
Like an owl with beady brown eyes.
Knock, Knock, Knock there's Mr Ellis,
He's at the door with a tie like a trellis
He comes in and talks to Mrs Inglis.
And he asks her "have you a minute".
They go outside and have a chat.
Mrs Inglis then comes in having a laugh.
Teachers I think they are like lions.
Looking for their prey to give a referral.
Teachers! Teachers! Teachers!
They arrive at school with bags of books
And walk to the staffroom to put their coats on hooks
Its 10 past 3 the school bell rings and the teachers sigh in great relief.
The children all smile as they leave for home.
As yet another day passes.

Anwen Thomas Year 7CA Age 12

## Maerdy School Days

Every morning when I go to school, I go to reg and its way over the edge.
The lessons start five past nine, hope the day doesn't waste its time.
The bell goes for break time, which wastes my time. Two more lessons to go now.
Waiting for the bell for dinnertime, dinner is precious for all us children.
The teachers have their food at a table of four,
Eating it fast like they've never seen it before.
The last two lessons are finished for now. It's ten past three and it's home time for me.
I've started walking home and I'm ready for my tea.

Dale Pike Year 8 Age 13 and Katy Lloyd Year 8 Age 13

The Maerdy Archive was formed by a group of local residents who consider that the history of Maerdy and the surrounding areas must not be lost. The Maerdy Archive collects photographs, letters, maps, plans, documents, books, post cards, invoices, tools, mining artefacts, newspapers, drawings, stories, certificates, membership records, tickets etc. We also mount displays and exhibitions, give lectures and make the collection available for education projects and research, and we have managed to produce some of our marketing materials and publications bilingually. If you are able to assist, please contact us on 01443 732073.

Left to right, back row: Rodney Kempton, Valerie Thomas, Kenneth Williams, Cullen Morris, Gethin Jones, Colin Marsh, Ray Carlotti. Front row: Edith Kempton, Jean Williams, Odyle Thomas, David Owen, Arwyn Williams, Glenys Edwards, Viv Anderson.

David Owen and The Maerdy Archive 2002

Ffurfiwyd Archif Maerdy gan frodorion y cylch oedd yn ystyried na dylid colli hanes Maerdy a'r cylch. Mae Archif Maerdy yn casglu lluniau, llythyron, mapiau, cynlluniau dogfennau, llyfrau, cardiau post, anfonebau, offer, creiriau mwyngloddio, papurau newydd, storïau, tystysgrifau, recordiau aelodaeth, ticedi ayb. Rydym hefyd yn cyflwyno arddangosfeydd, darlithiau ac yn darparu mynediad i'r archif i ymchwilwyr a phrosiectau addysgol. Rydym wedi llwyddo cynhyrchu deunydd marchnata a chyhoeddiadau dwyieithog. Os gallwch fod o gymorth cysylltwch â 01443 732073.

Chwith i'r dde, rhes gefn: Rodney Kempton, Valerie Thomas, Kenneth Williams, Cullen Morris, Gethin Jones, Colin Marsh, Ray Carlotti. Rhes flaen: Edith Kempton, Jean Williams, Odyle Thomas, David Owen, Arwyn Williams, Glenys Edwards, Viv Anderson.

David Owen ac Archif Maerdy 2002

Rhondda History
Mardy
Schools